Elmer A. Ruff was born February 6th, 1931, in Secane, Pennsylvania. Later that same year, his family moved to Cincinnati, Ohio. He was homeschooled until his freshman year in high school. He then attended Withrow High School. In 1950, he began work on his undergraduate degree; he graduated from the University of Cincinnati in 1955 with both a Bachelor of Applied Arts Degree and a Bachelor of Science in Education Degree. He then completed work on his Master of Fine Arts Degree from the University of Florida in 1956.

Elmer won numerous awards and honors in college, such as winning First Prize for his Senior Thesis and being selected as Grand Marshal in his undergraduate graduation ceremony. He was awarded two non-resident tuition scholarships at the University of Florida, was offered but declined a Fulbright Scholarship to England, and was selected to be a member of Delta Phi Delta, a National Art Honorary, and Kappa Delta Phi, a National Education Honorary.

Elmer's teaching experiences include the following: instructor of evening college, University of Cincinnati; instructor of weekend classes, Cincinnati Art Museum; instructor, Cincinnati Junior League; instructor, adult education classes, Madeira High School; and instructor of private art classes for over fifty years in Cincinnati, Troy, and Lebanon, Ohio.

He has had dozens of one-man shows and group exhibitions in various states such as New York, Michigan, New Jersey, Missouri, Montana, Indiana, Iowa, Florida, Kentucky, and Tennessee.

Elmer's works have been reviewed in numerous publications, including *Art News*, *The Arts*, *La Review Moderne* (Paris), the *Cincinnati Enquirer*, *St. Louis Post-Dispatch*, and *Dayton Journal Herald*, among others.

In his personal life, Elmer was married to his wonderful better half, Ellen Jane (Lohr) Ruff, for almost 52 years until her passing in 2016.

He has several impressive collections of bottles, cigar bands, and marbles. He is also a devotee of music, especially classical, and he enjoys doing yardwork when the weather permits (although the yardwork might be a thinly veiled excuse for smoking a good cigar, one of his other great passions!).

This book is a combination of E. A. Ruff's artwork and his philosophy on art, and at times, life in general. As the reader proceeds through this book, he/she can find his statements about art and life on the left hand page and an example of his artwork on the right. The two pages, left and right, are not necessarily tied together in any fashion.

Part 1

Assemblages

"Assemblage, in art, work produced by the incorporation of everyday objects into the composition.
Although each non-art object, such as a piece of rope or newspaper, acquires aesthetic or symbolic meanings within the context of the whole work, it may retain something of its original identity. The term assemblage, as coined by the artist Jean Dubuffet in the 1950s, may refer to both planar and three-dimensional constructions."
- The Editors of Encyclopædia Britannica

*

Always paint from thin to thick.
Allow to dry between layers.
Keep it simple in the beginning.
Work toward detail.
Try to maintain a level surface weight.

*

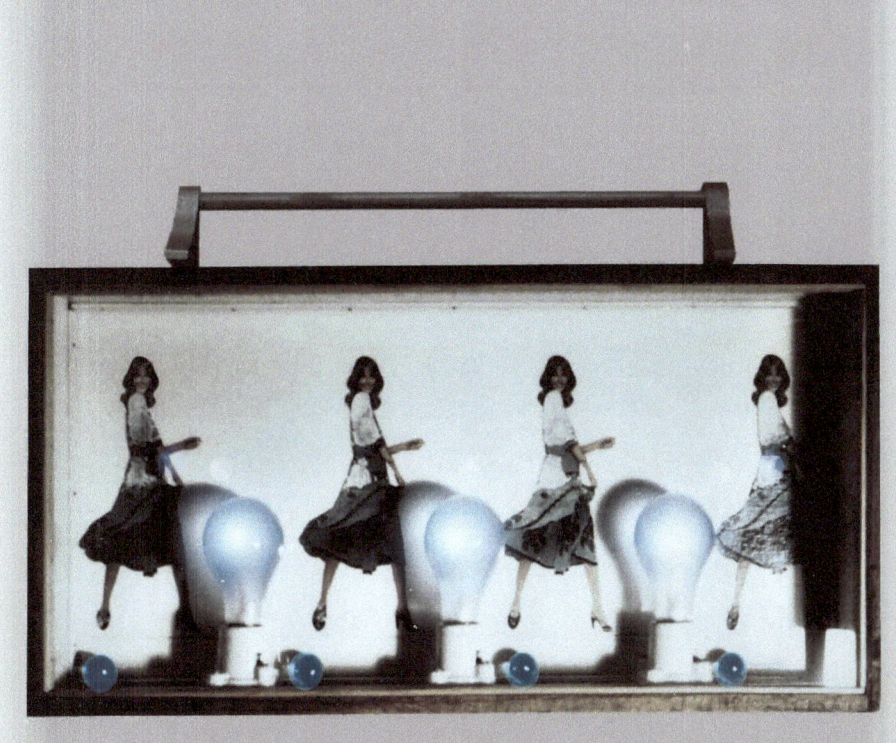

Blaue Elf

1.

*

Surface weight is a psychological term.
It refers to how simple or complex the paint structure is.
Think of the difference between silk and burlap.
The term depends upon such factors as paint
thickness, complex color structure, color
saturation, texture, pattern, etc.
The point is, surface weight should be
kept the same throughout the painting.
*

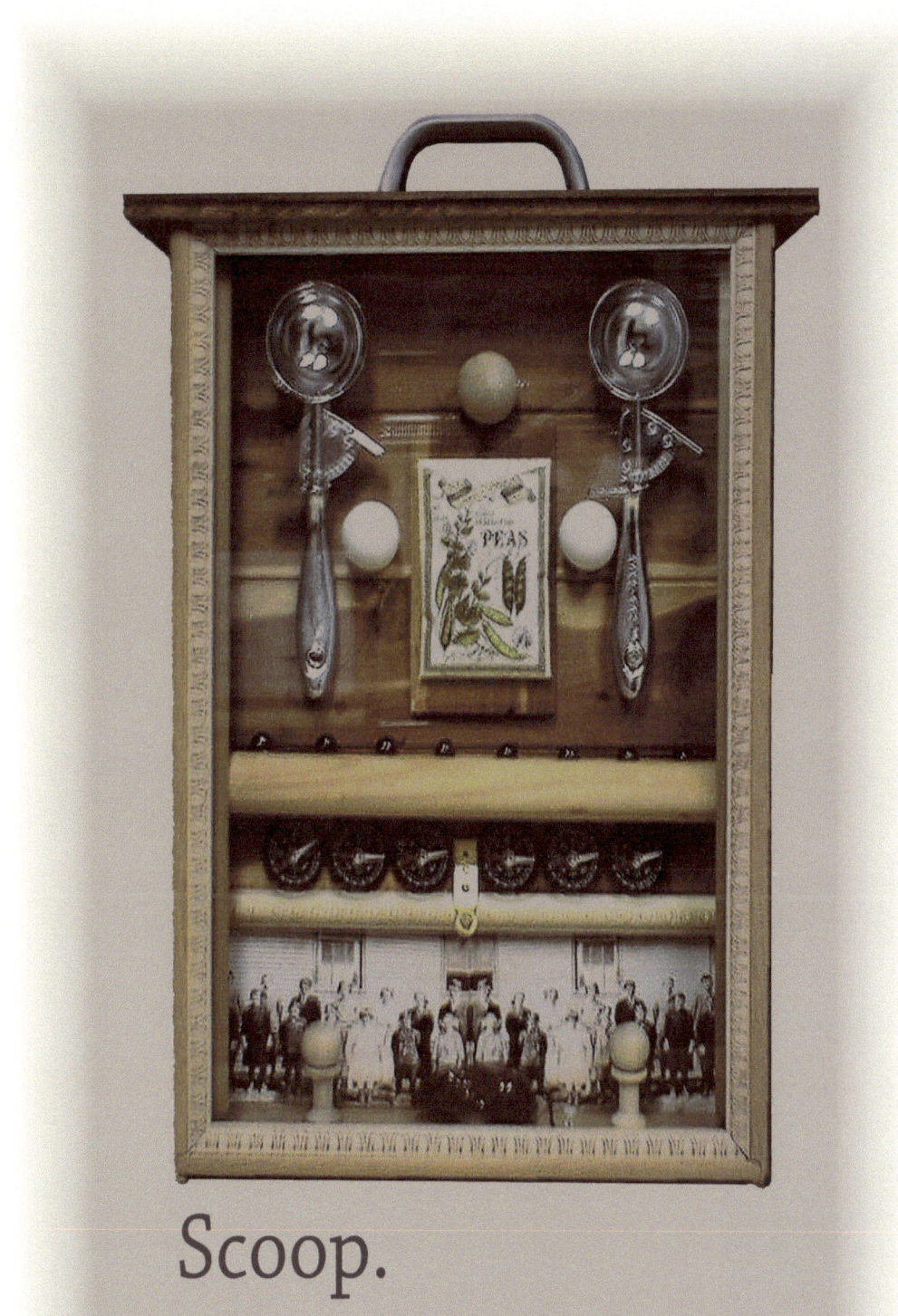

Scoop.

2.

*

**Paint the deepest planes first and
then work toward those nearest to you.
When painting indirectly (i.e., in many layers),
repeat the process.**

*

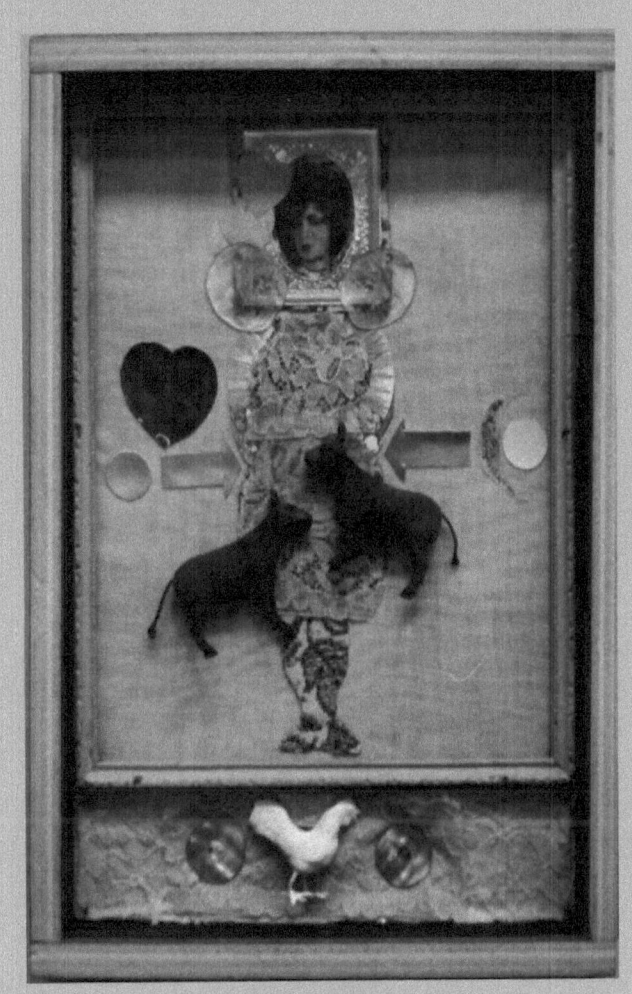

Mule Box

3.

*

**Use the same technique or techniques
throughout the entire painting.
Avoid the localization of a specific
alternate technique.**

*

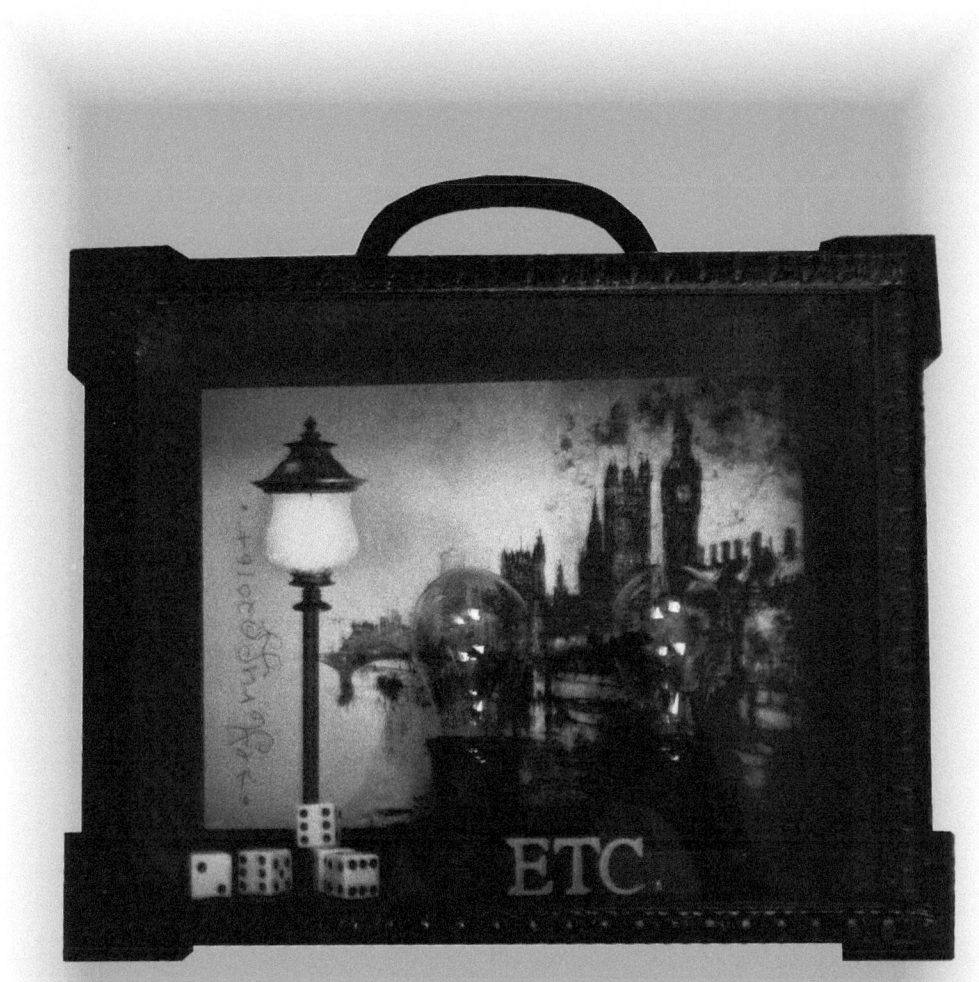

London .

4.

*

**Indirect paintings (many layers) are more
natural, aesthetically richer, full of
subtleties, and build a better model of reality.
They are more challenging to both
the painter and the viewer.**

*

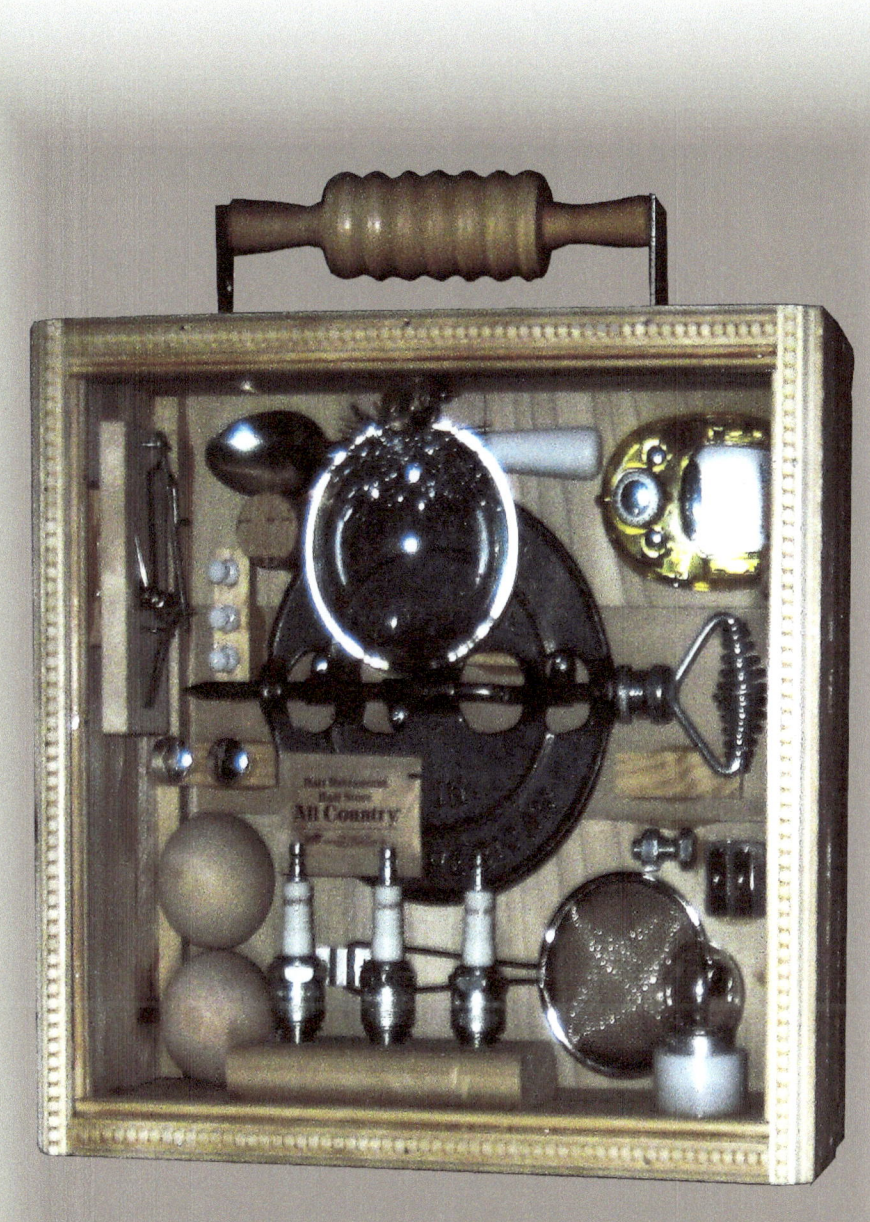

Work Shop Salad..

5.

*

Do not develop the habit of leaving paintings unfinished.
If your interest diminishes, wait a while and continue later.
If your motivation for a particular painting fails,
you may have to invent a new one.
This is possible.

*

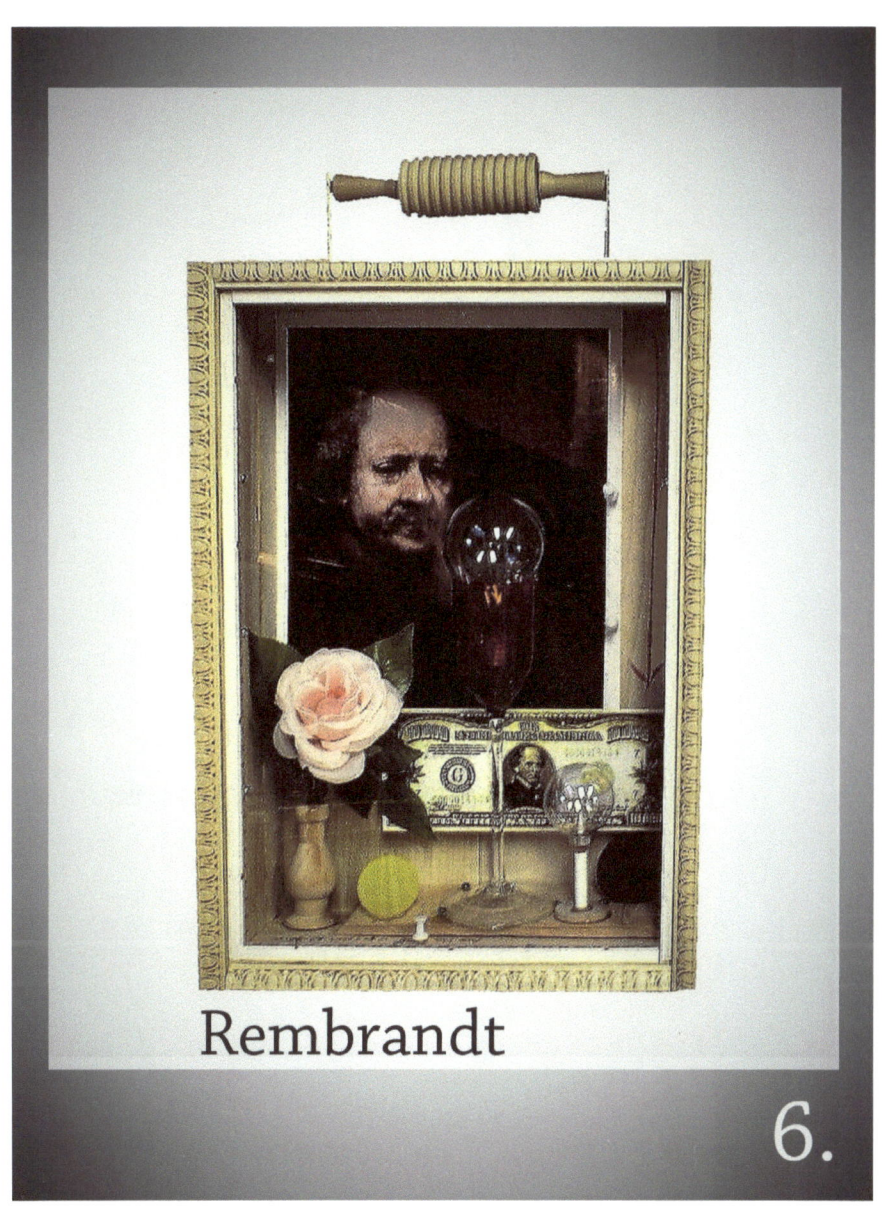

Rembrandt

6.

*

**The primary purpose of illustration
is to tell a story or to be descriptive.**

*

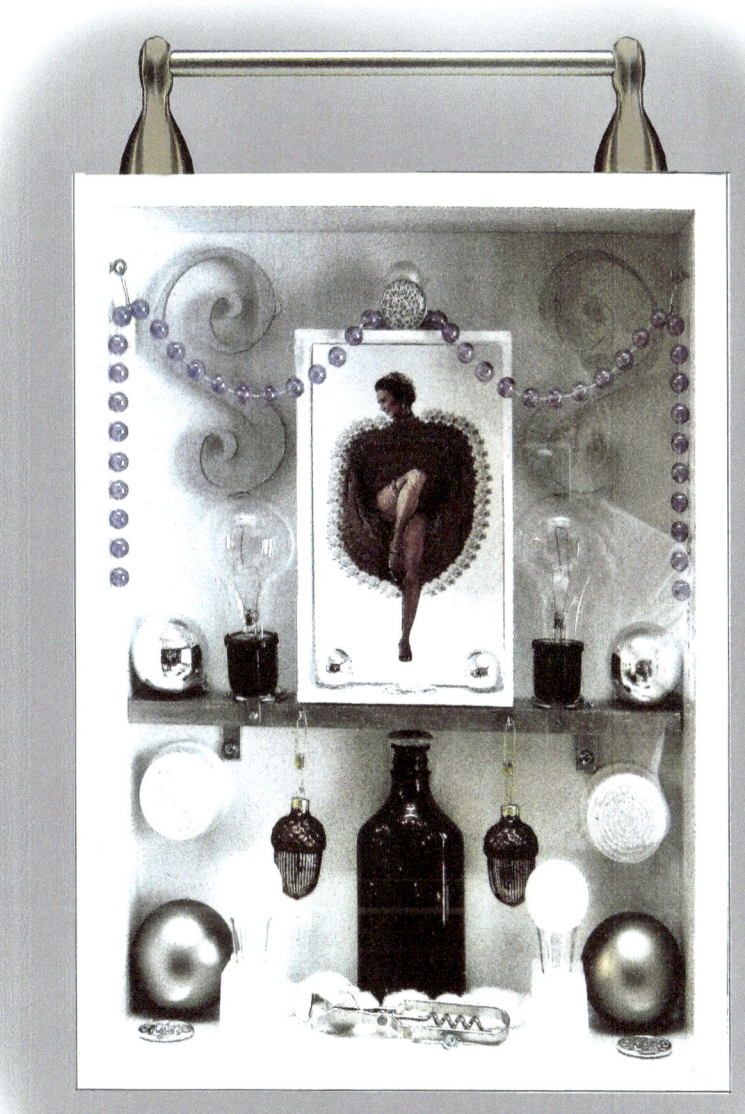

Can Can.

7.

*

**Do not destroy a work in a fit of passion;
make a sober judgment some time later.
We make poor decisions when
frustrated and fatigued.**

*

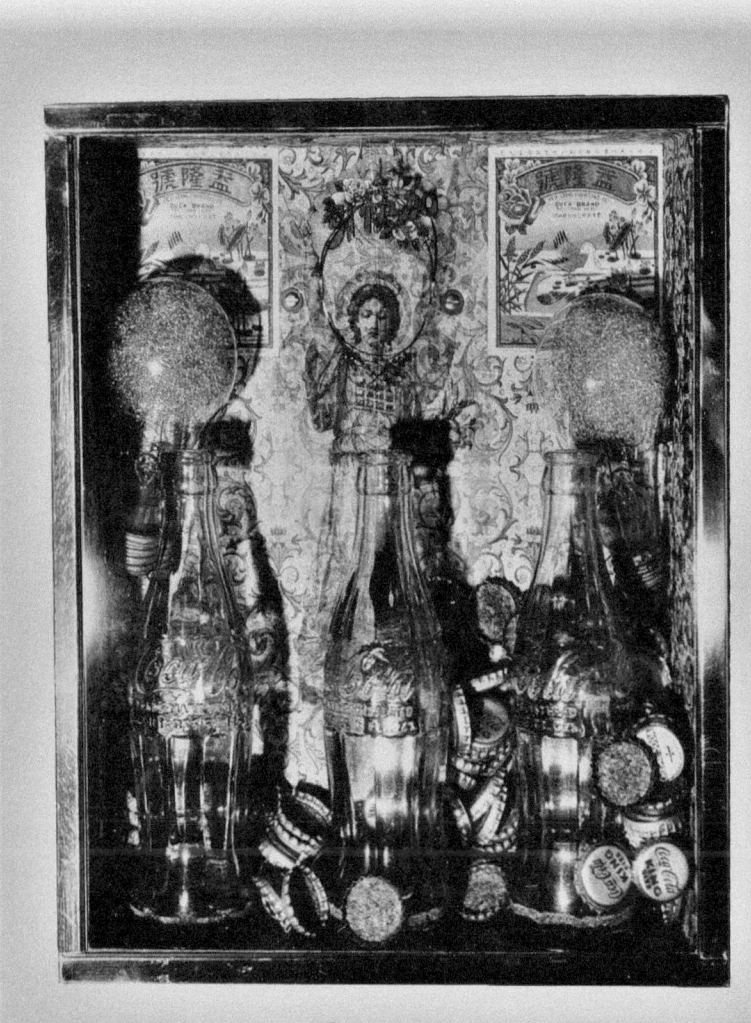

Coke, plus.

8.

*

**Try to avoid reworking old paintings.
They represent a valid statement
for a particular time in an artist's development.
If you must, paint a second version of the subject.**

*

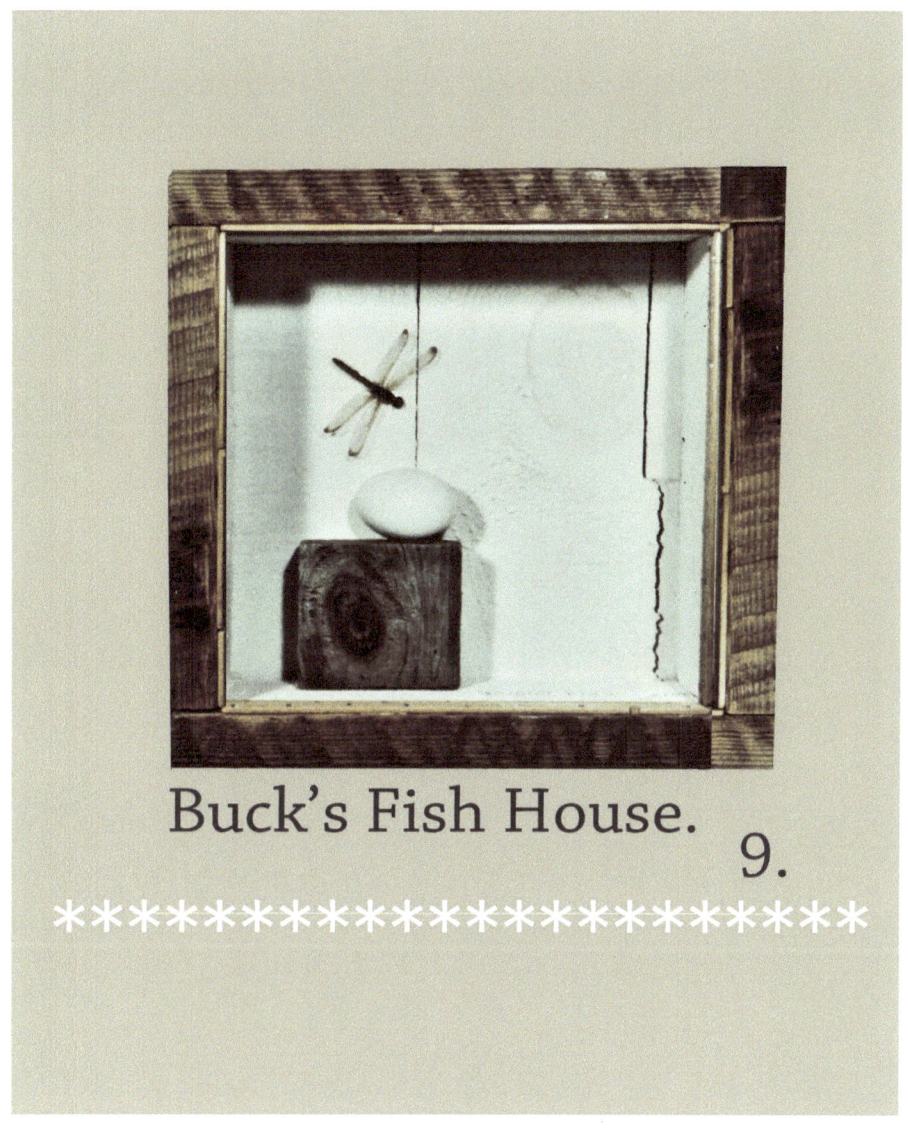

Buck's Fish House.

9.

****

*

Always accept yourself and what you are able to achieve.
Do not try to emulate another artist simply
because you admire him or her.
Great painters have always been honest about who they are.
Copies are seldom better than the original.

*

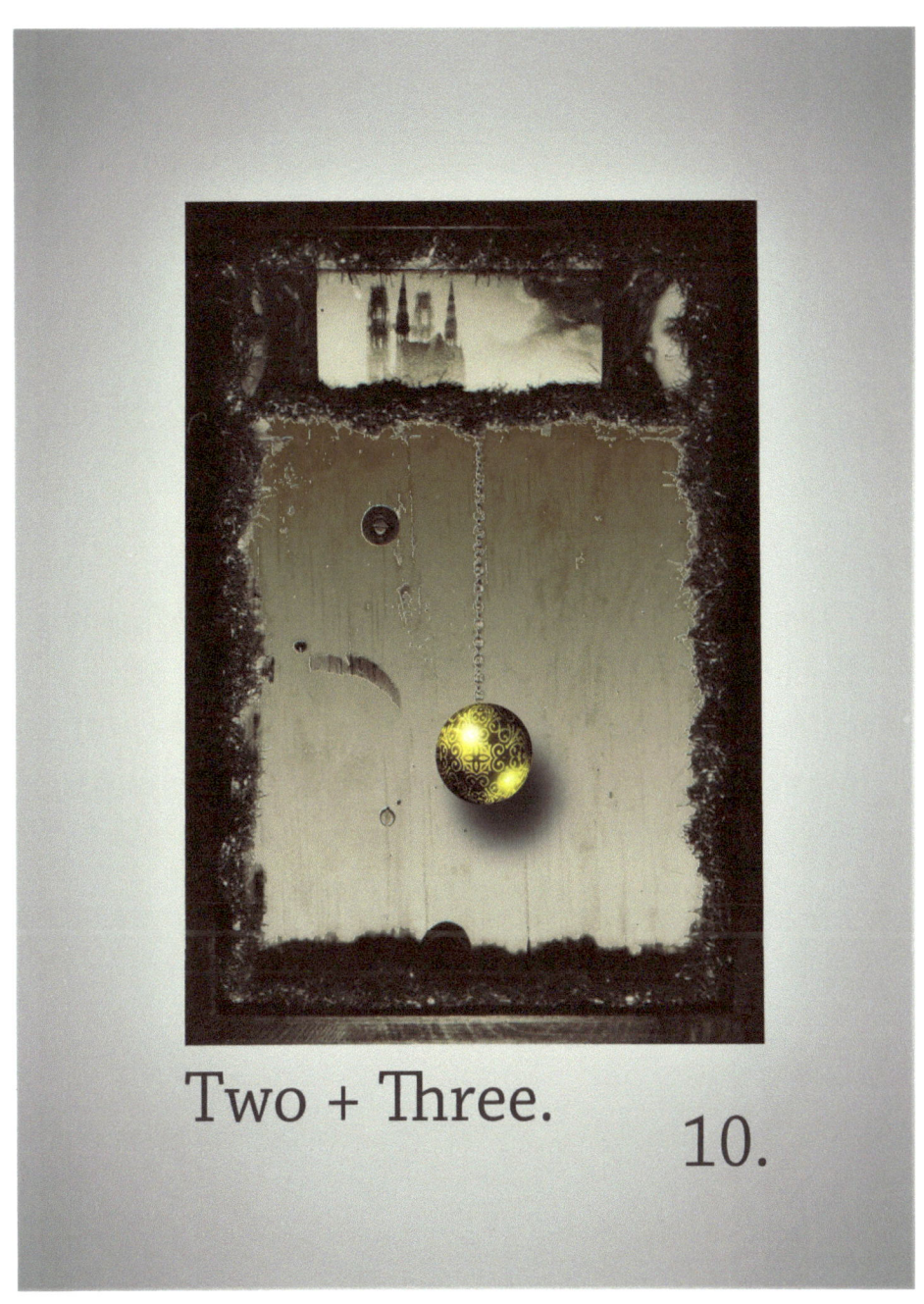

Two + Three.

10.

*

**The most precious thing about each of us is
that which makes us different from all others.
Wanting to be someone else is a sign of emptiness.
In our desire to be accepted, we often deny our
true identities; this is a serious mistake.
Lookalikes are soon forgotten!**

*

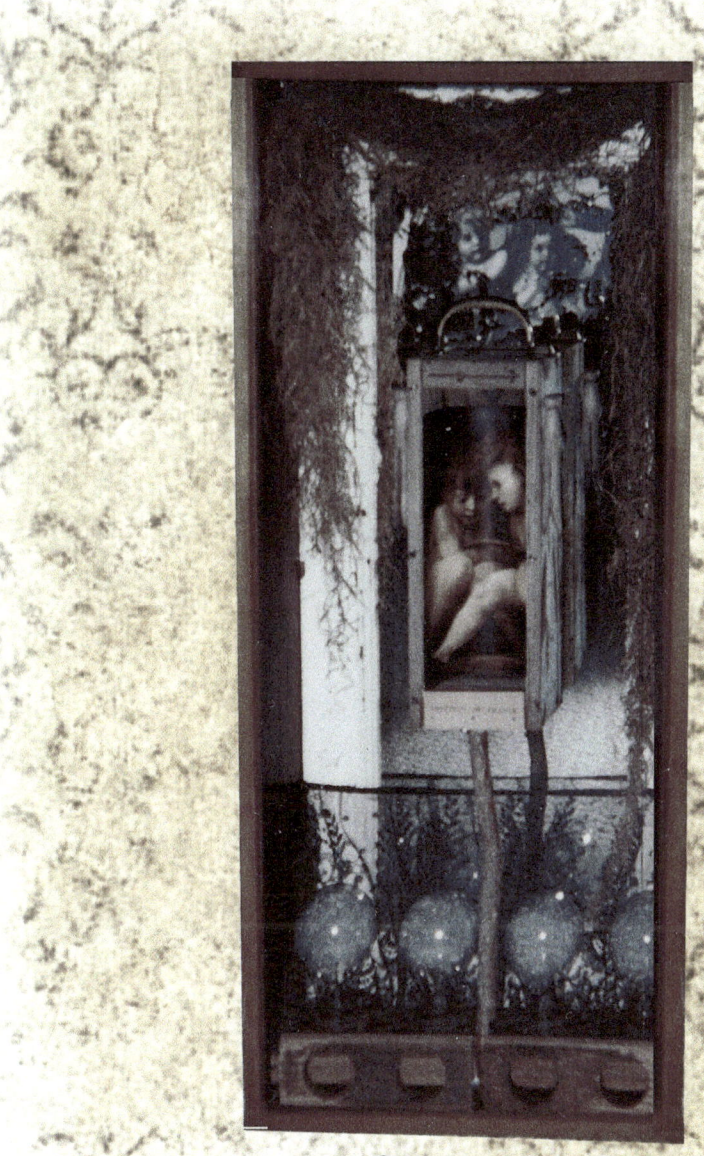

Madison.

11.

*

Always please yourself first, have strong convictions, and avoid being frustrated by the adverse opinions of others. Remember that a giraffe is a horse designed by a committee.

*

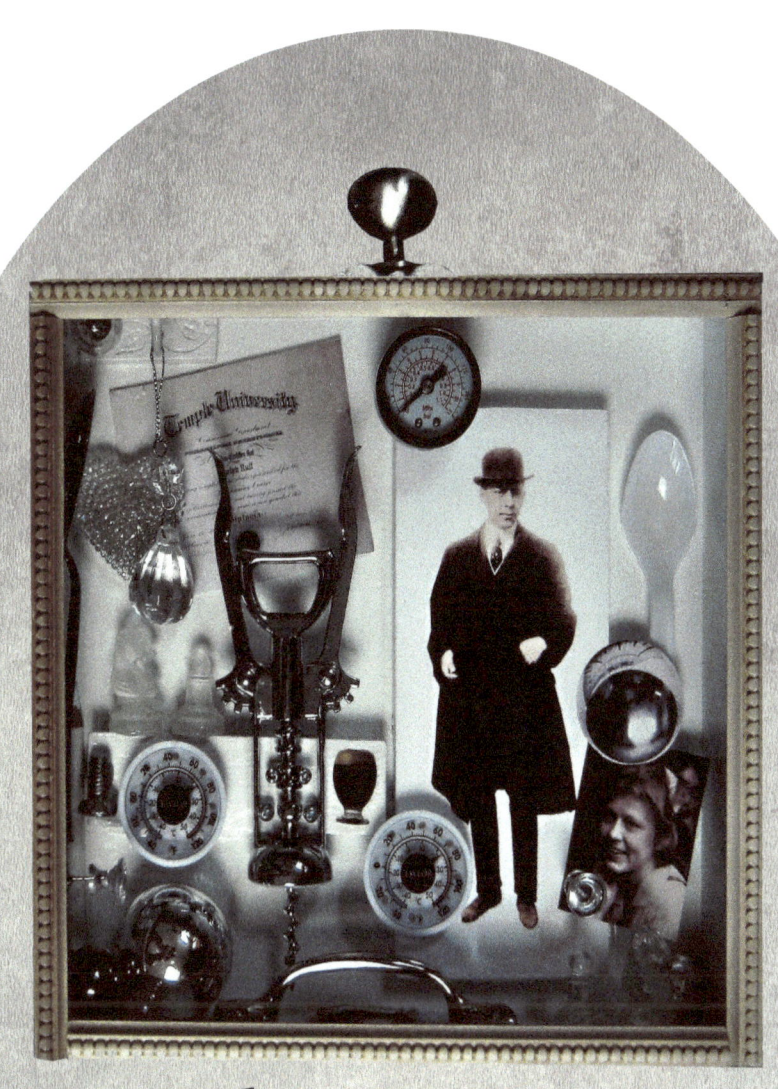

Temple.   12.

*

Always be sincere.

*

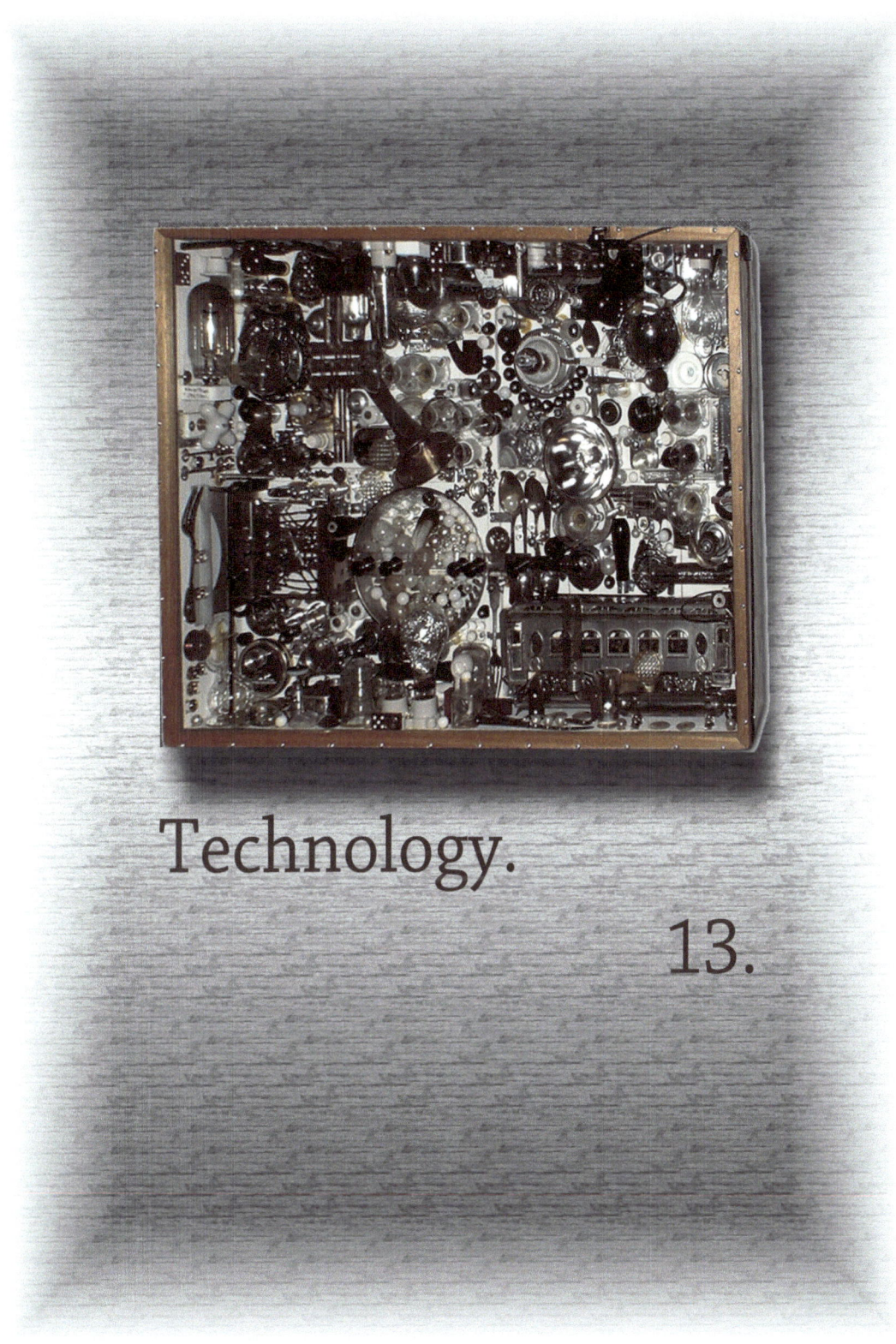

Technology.

13.

*

Skill and facility are but a means; they should
not be considered an end in themselves.
Pyrotechnics are impressive but not profound.
There is a wide audience for a skillful performance.
Remember that nothing, even said
exquisitely, still amounts to nothing.
Skill should serve a higher purpose.
An idiot shaved, given a haircut, and dressed
in a fine business suit is still an idiot.

*

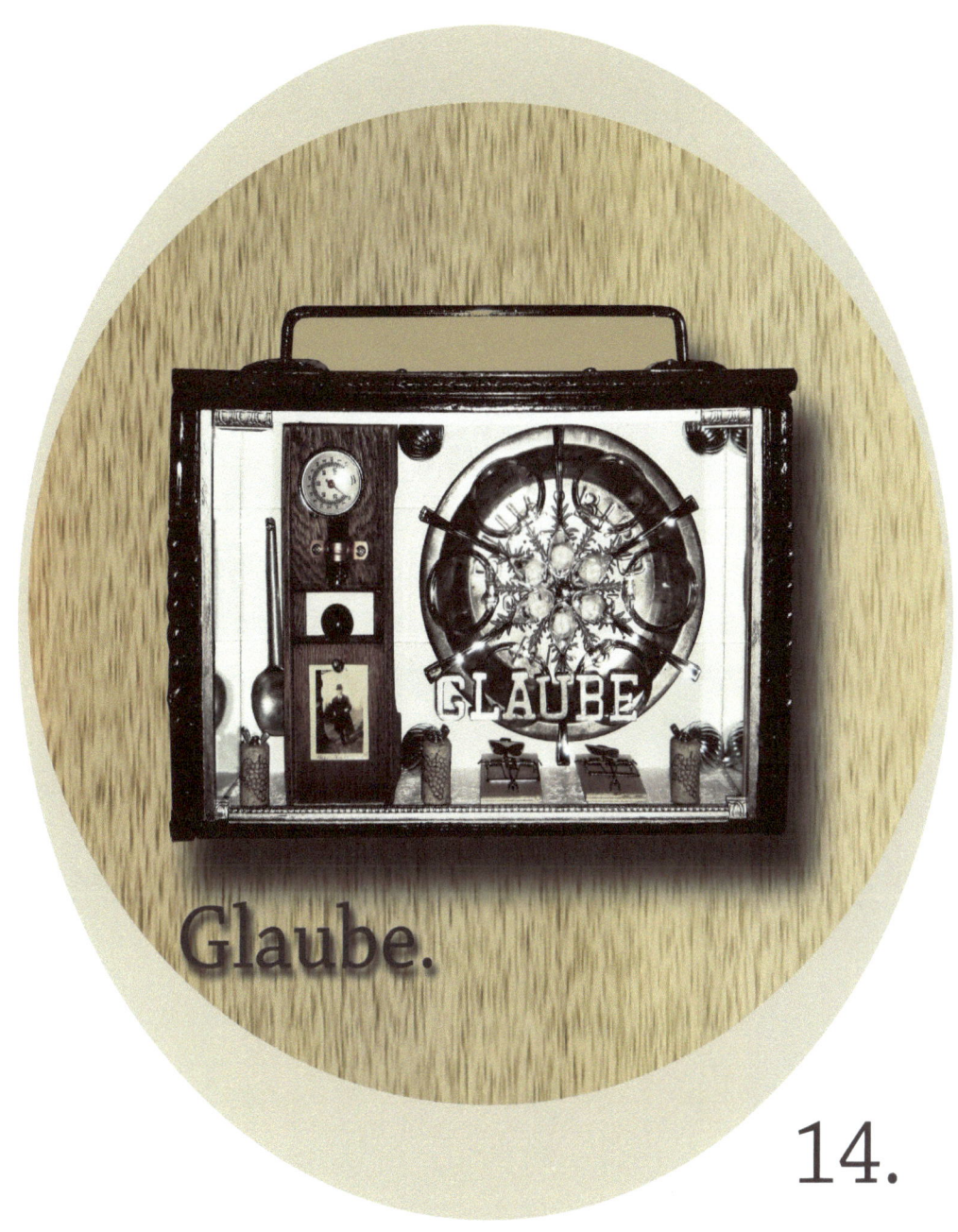

Glaube.

14.

*

**Great paintings contain emotionally
provoking or evoking qualities.
They are the products of insight, intuition,
sensitivity, aesthetic maturity, understanding,
a love of medium, and passion.**

*

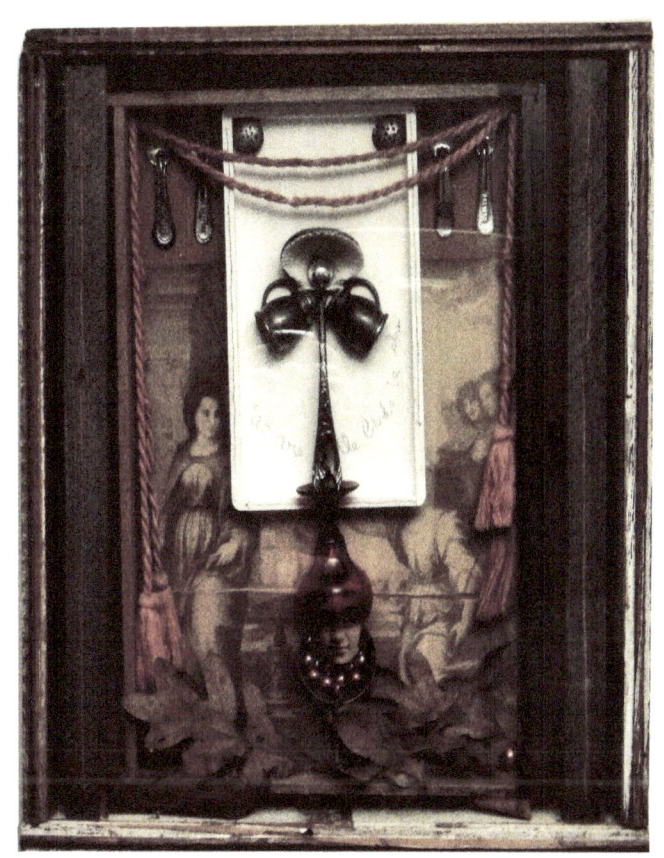

Goblet.

15.

*

**Subject matter should be focused on things that
you know, love, and have personally experienced.
Never attempt to paint something
that you fail to understand or know.
Empathy endows a painting with the spirit of its subject.
This is not a mechanical procedure.**

*

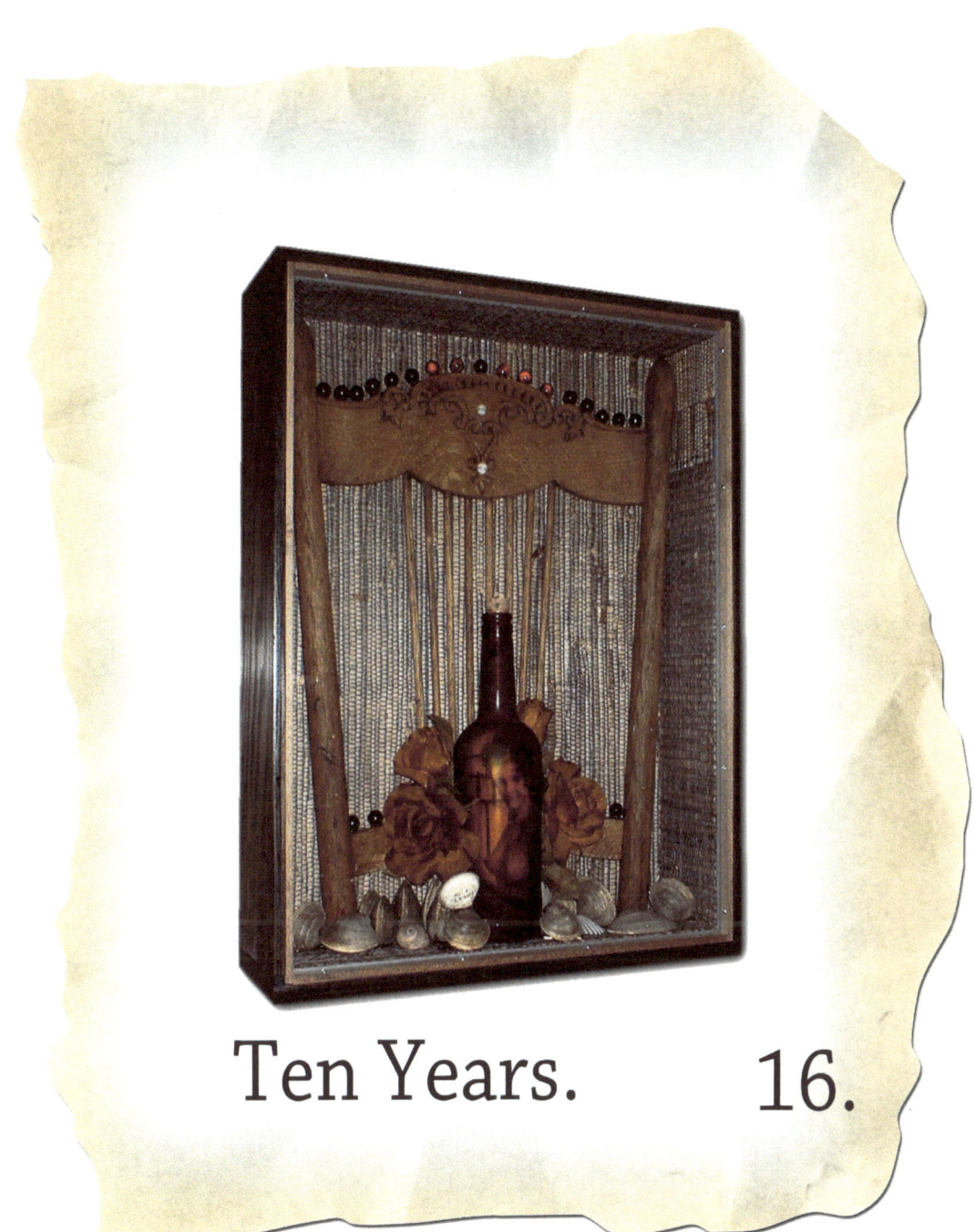

Ten Years.   16.

*

**Thoroughly understand, be sensitive to, enjoy,
and have a passion for your chosen medium.**

*

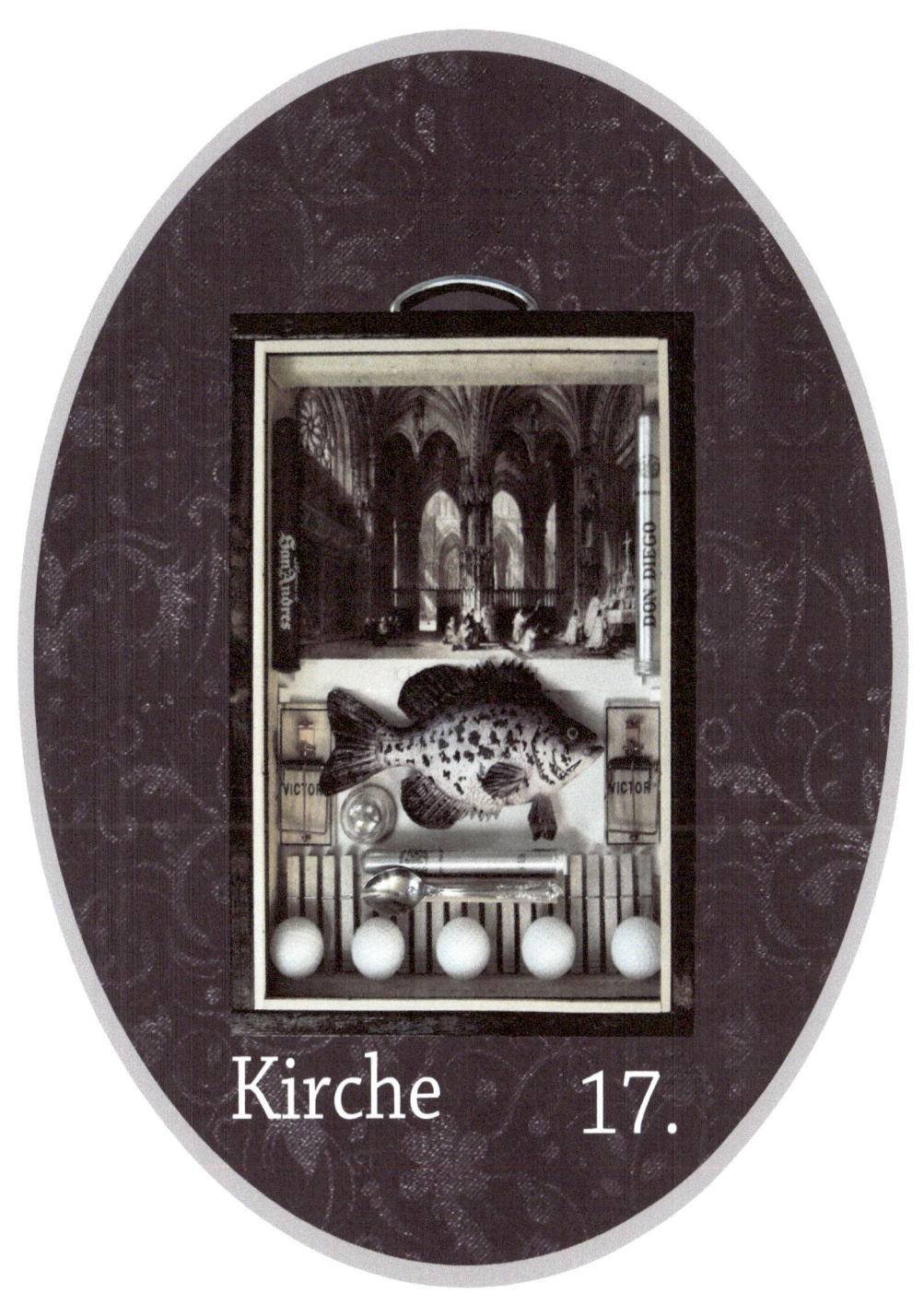

Kirche 17.

*

**It is wise to work with an
alternate medium from time to time.
If you are an oil painter, you might consider
working in pastels as an alternate material.
Another example would be a watercolor artist trying acrylics.**

*

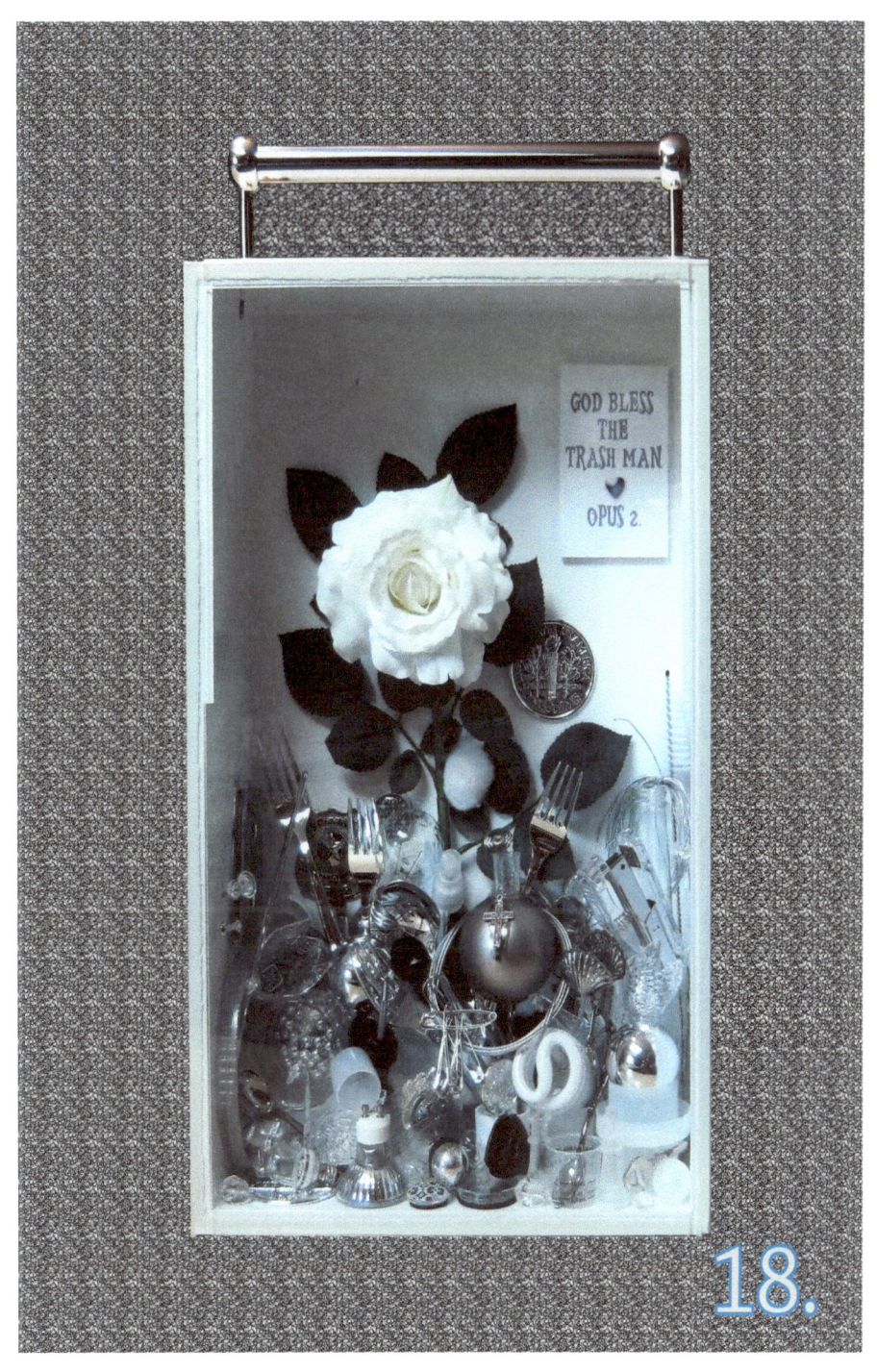

GOD BLESS
THE
TRASH MAN
♥
OPUS 2.

18.

Trash Man.

*

**Remember, it is better to do a few things
well than to do everything mediocre –
or worse yet, do everything poorly!**

*

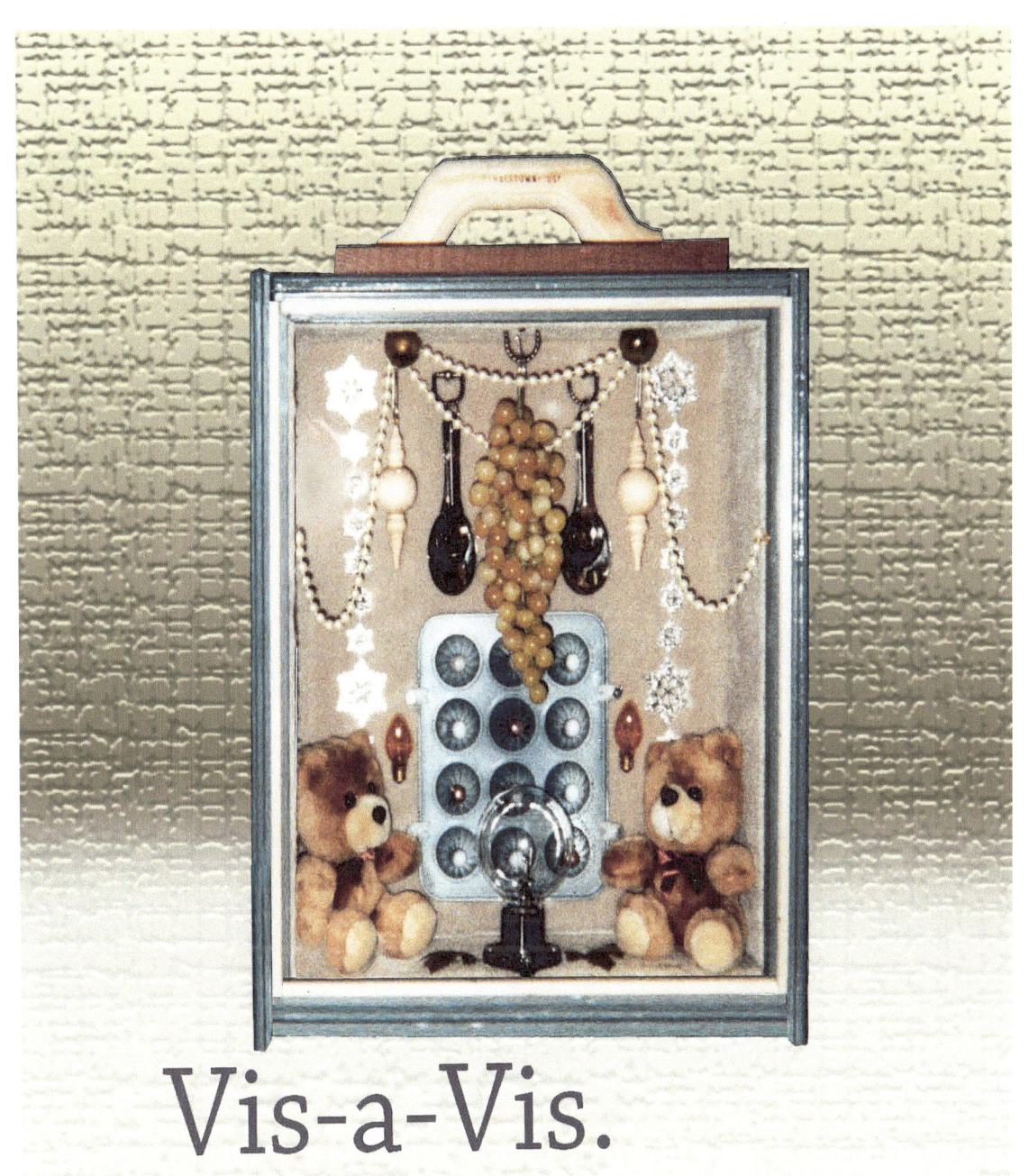

Vis-a-Vis.

19.

*

**It is wise to limit subject matter,
media, palette, and so forth.
By so doing, we become more effective.**

*

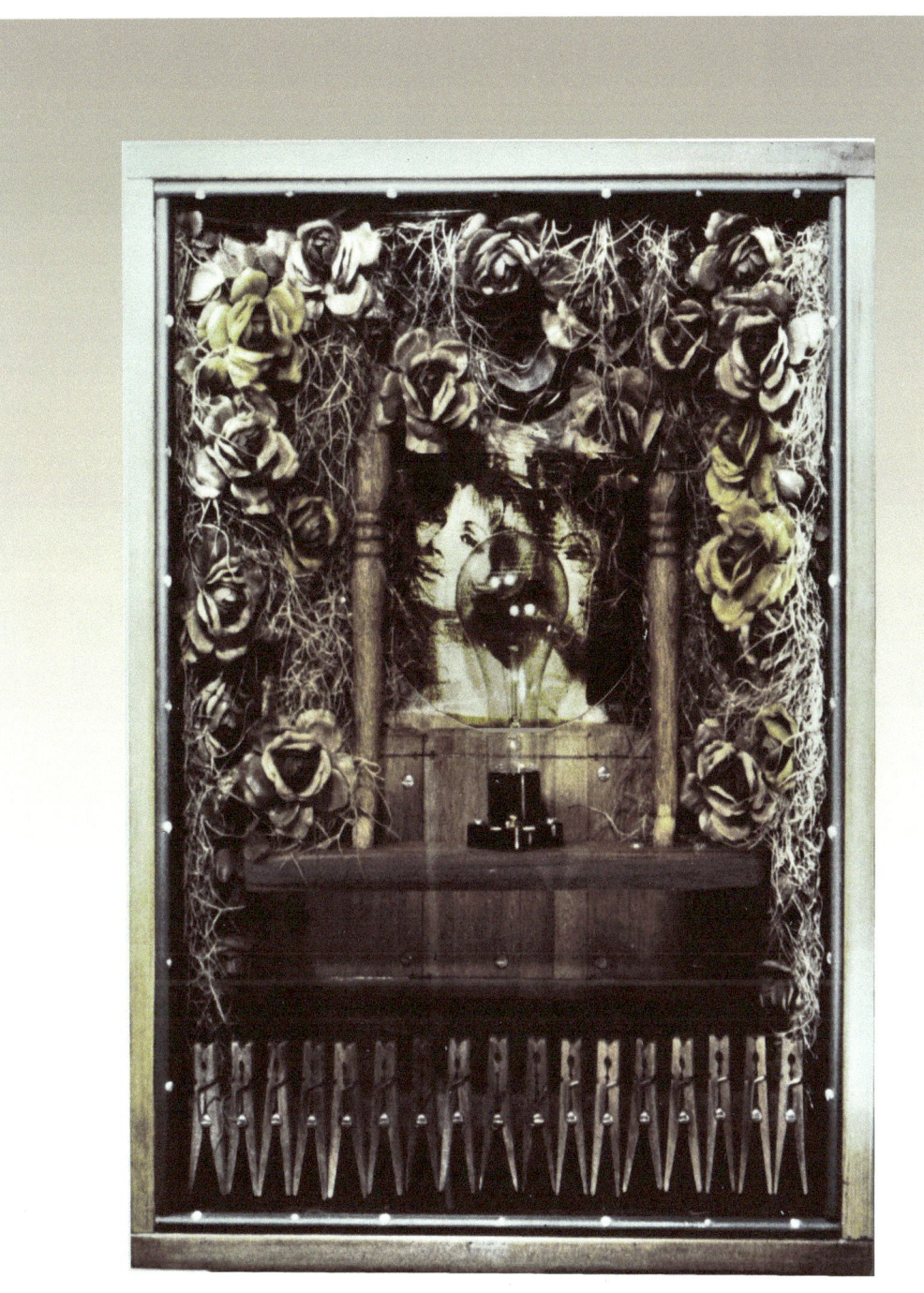

Rustic Box.

20.

*

Try to build an inner strength; do not let what
others think prevent you from being yourself.
We have the right to express ourselves as long
as we accept responsibility for what we do.
My personal view is that art must
be both positive and beautiful.
In this regard, I have reservations regarding
political art, as it places emphasis upon
content as opposed to aesthetics.

*

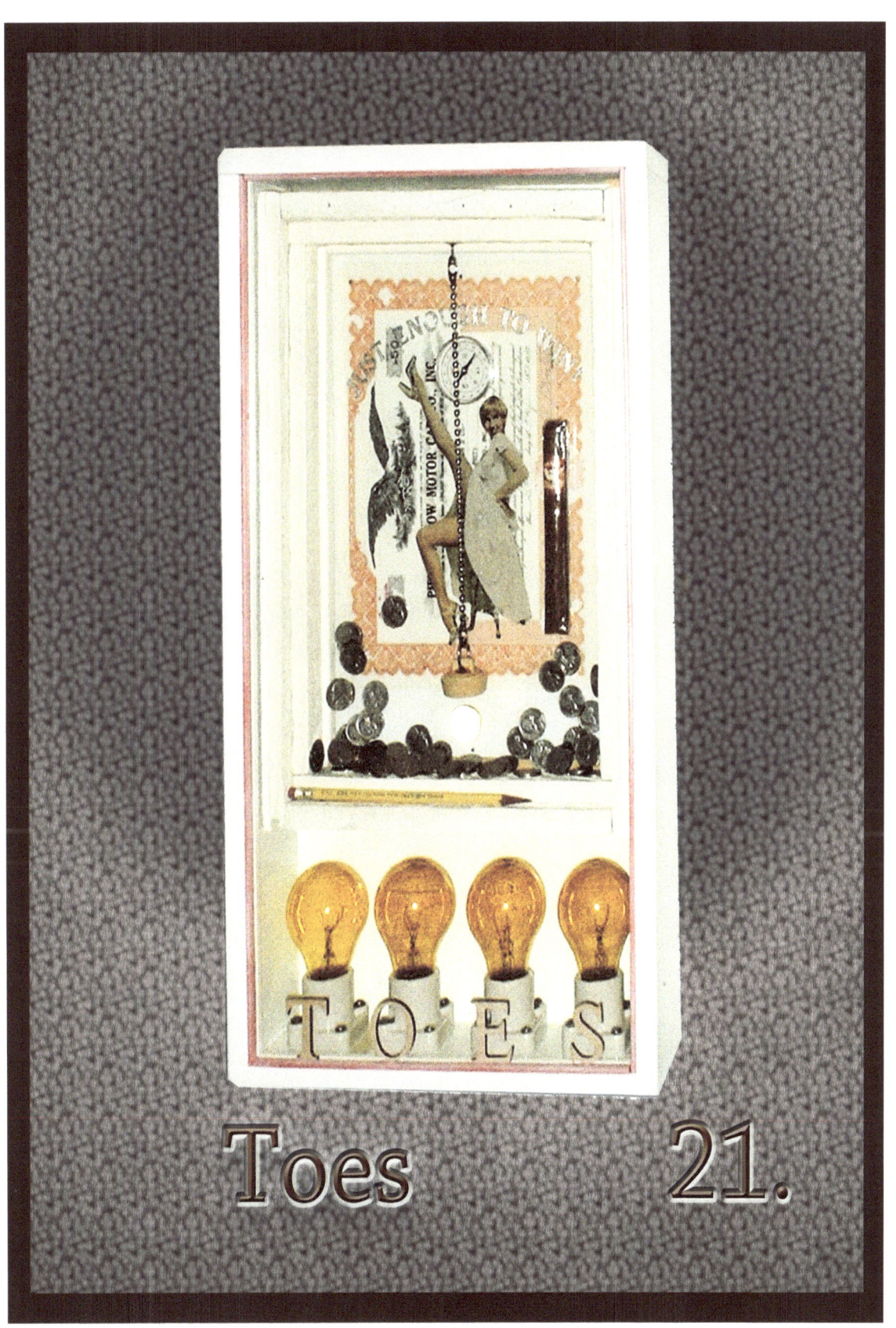

Toes   21.

*

**Paint at home as well as in class.
The most effective way to learn how
to paint is simply to paint and
paint and paint and paint.
Practice always exceeds theory.**

*

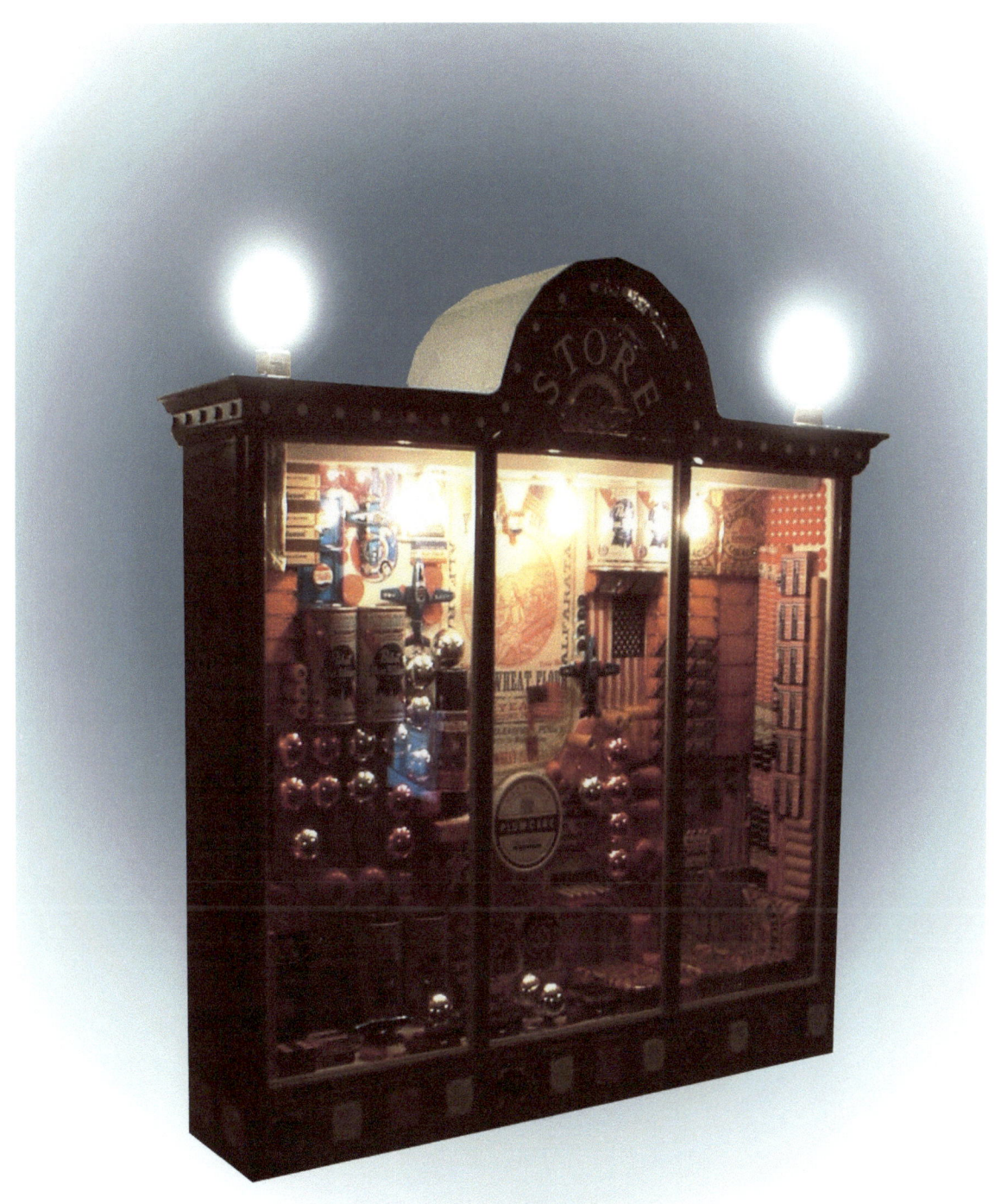

July 4TH.

22.

*

Try to relax and have fun during class.
Often, we do our best work when relaxed and automatic.
Rigid behavior produces lifeless,
rigid paintings and destroys feelings.
When we enjoy what we are doing,
we always do a better job.
This applies to every profession.

*

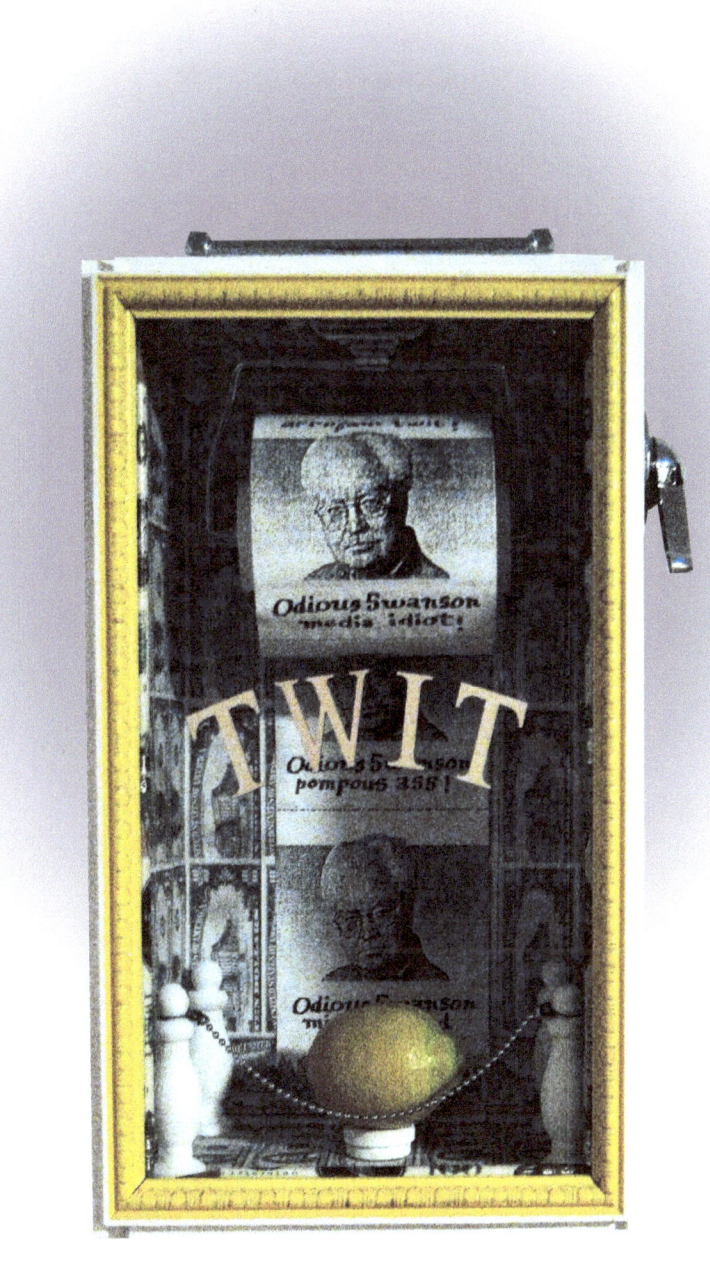

TWIT.   23.

*

**Commercial art stresses selling a product —
and sometimes even itself.**

*

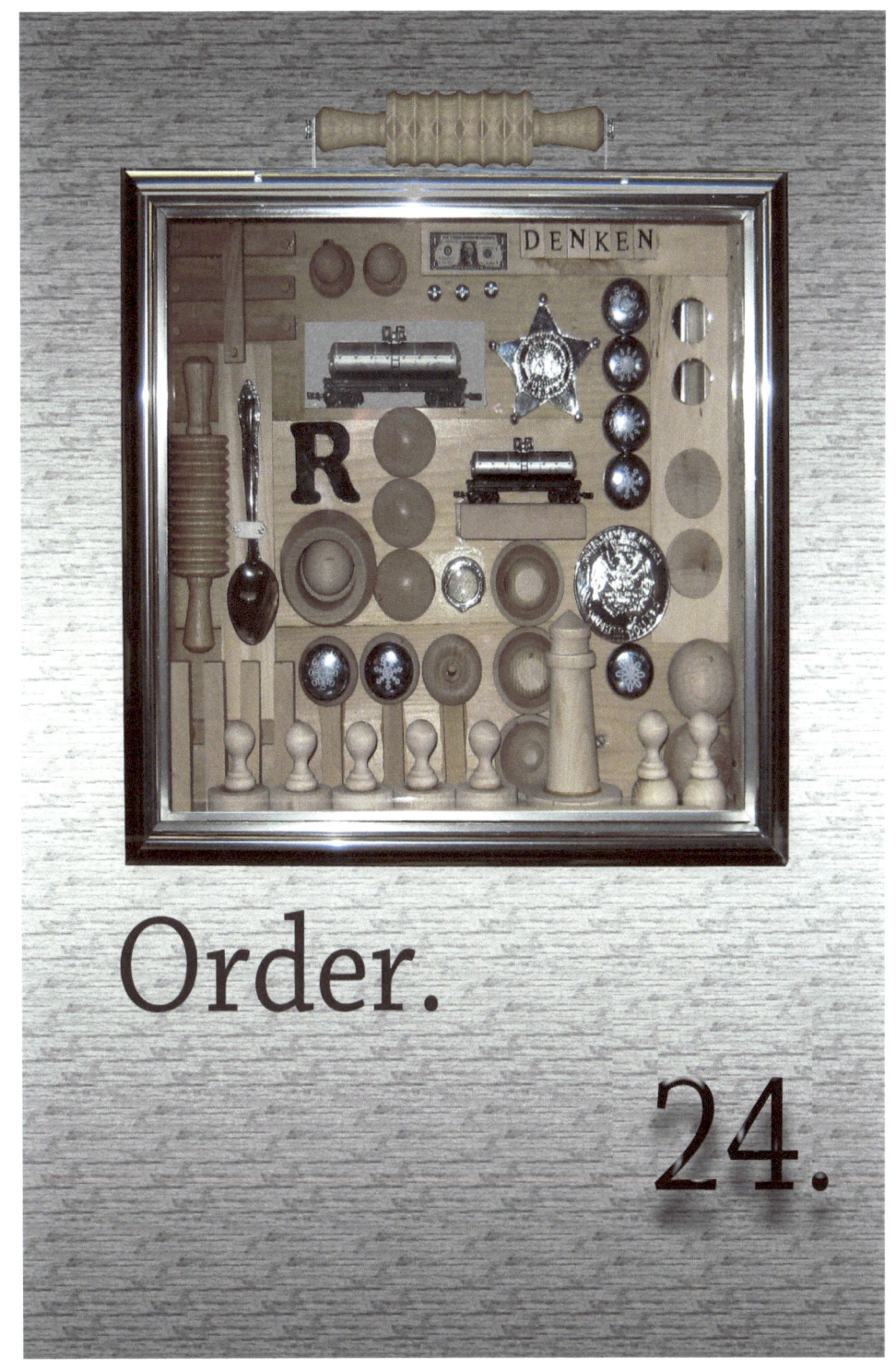

Order.

24.

Part 2

Mixed Media, Watercolors, Collages, Oils, Acrylics, and Digital Art

"Mixed media" tends to refer to a work of visual art that combines various traditionally distinct visual art media — for example, a work on canvas that combines paint, ink, and collage could properly be called a "mixed media" work, not a work of "multimedia art."

Collage is a piece of art made by attaching various materials such as photographs and pieces of paper or fabric onto a backing.

*

All water base media dry evenly.
Oil paints are different.
The various colors dry at different rates.

*

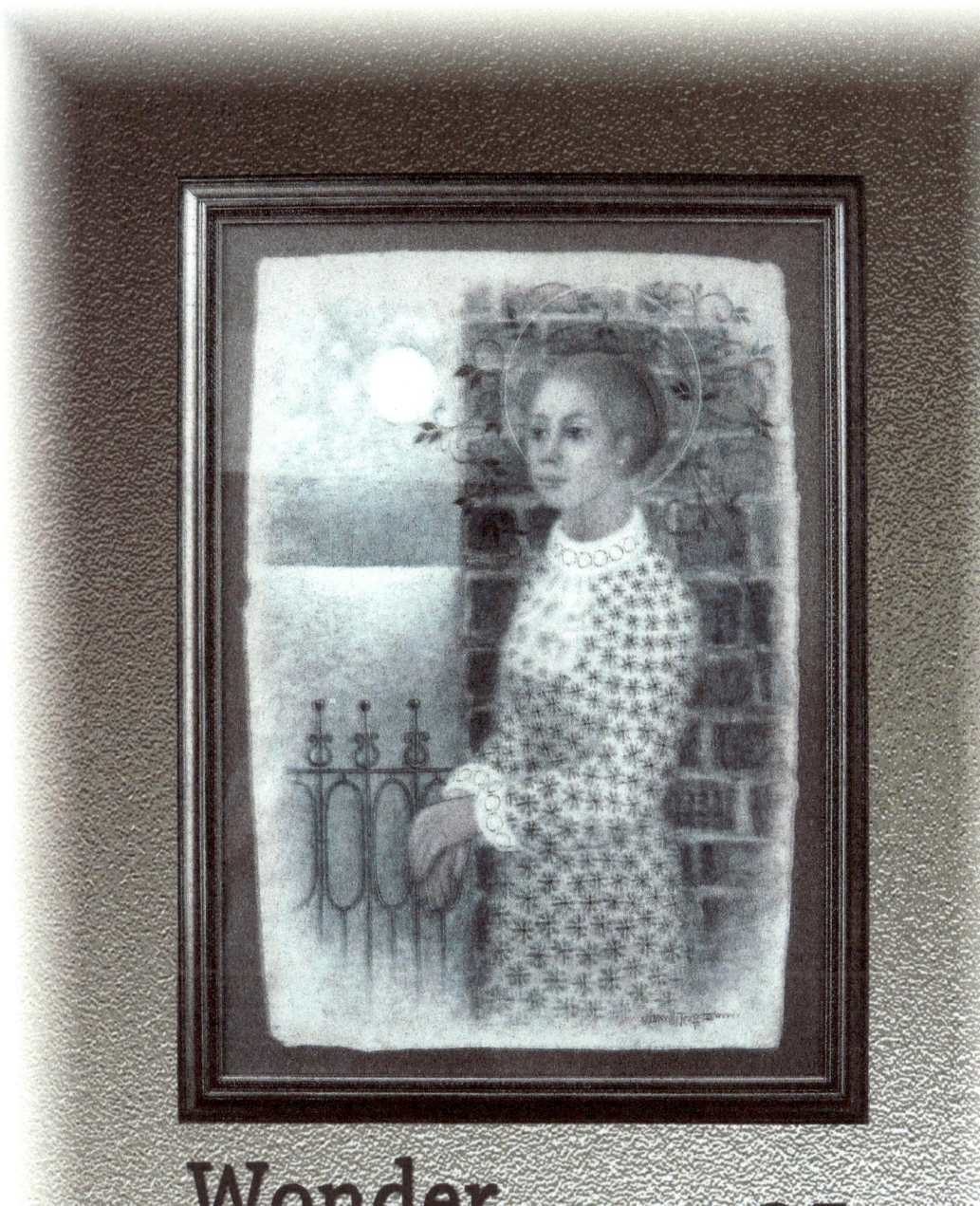

Wonder.
Mixed Media.

25.

*

A professional artist makes a living in art. This does not necessarily mean that such a person produces top-quality work. Mediocrity dominates every profession.

*

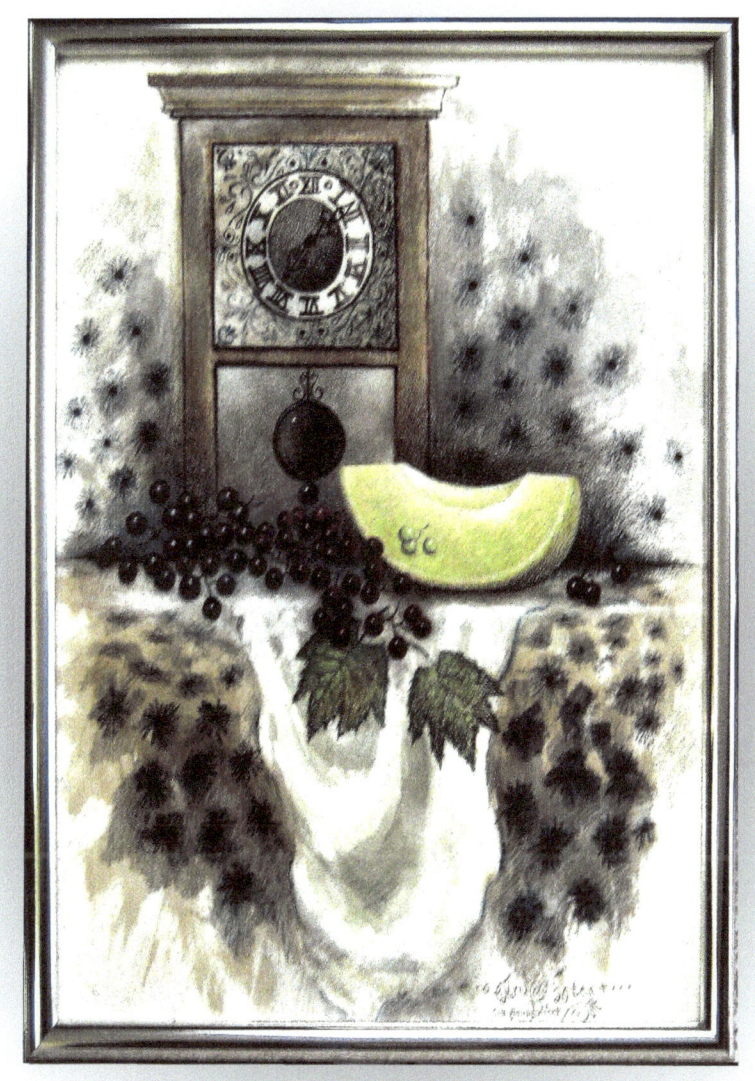

Still life.   26.
Mixed Media.

*

**It is far better to be a legitimate
artist than merely to look like one.
It is wrong to be an artist ostensibly;
it is wrong to be anything ostensibly.**

*

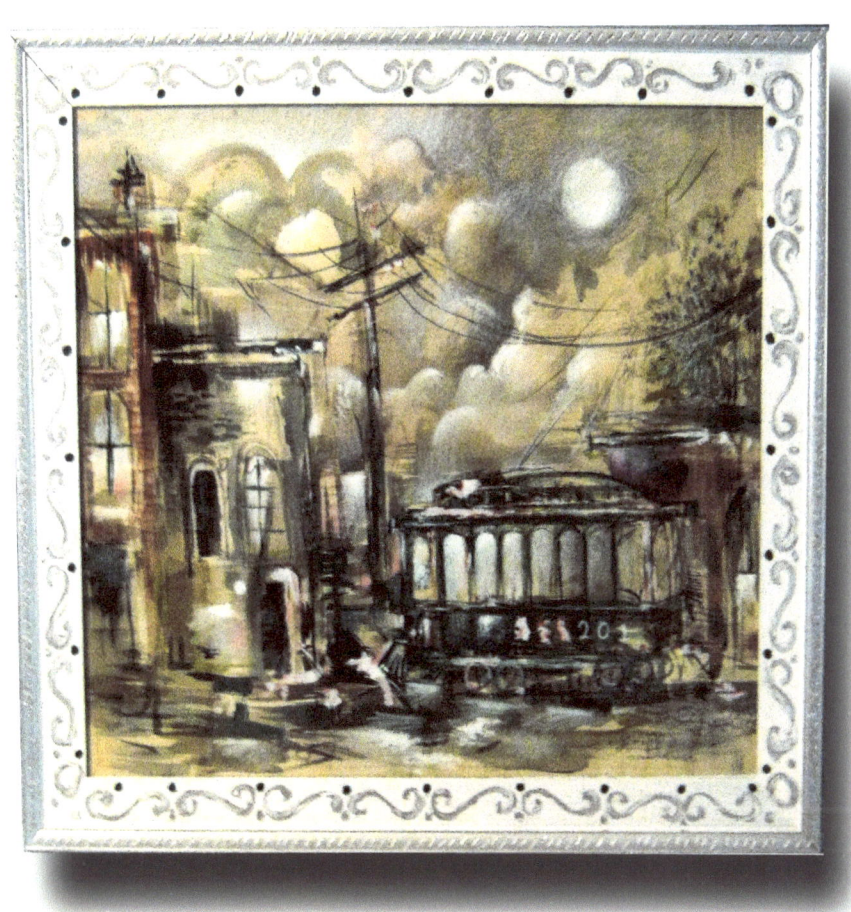

Street Car.
Mixed Media.

27.

*

**Persons seeking power, visibility, and
wealth through fine art are artists
for all the wrong reasons.
I am a painter [artist] simply
because that is what I wish to be.**

*

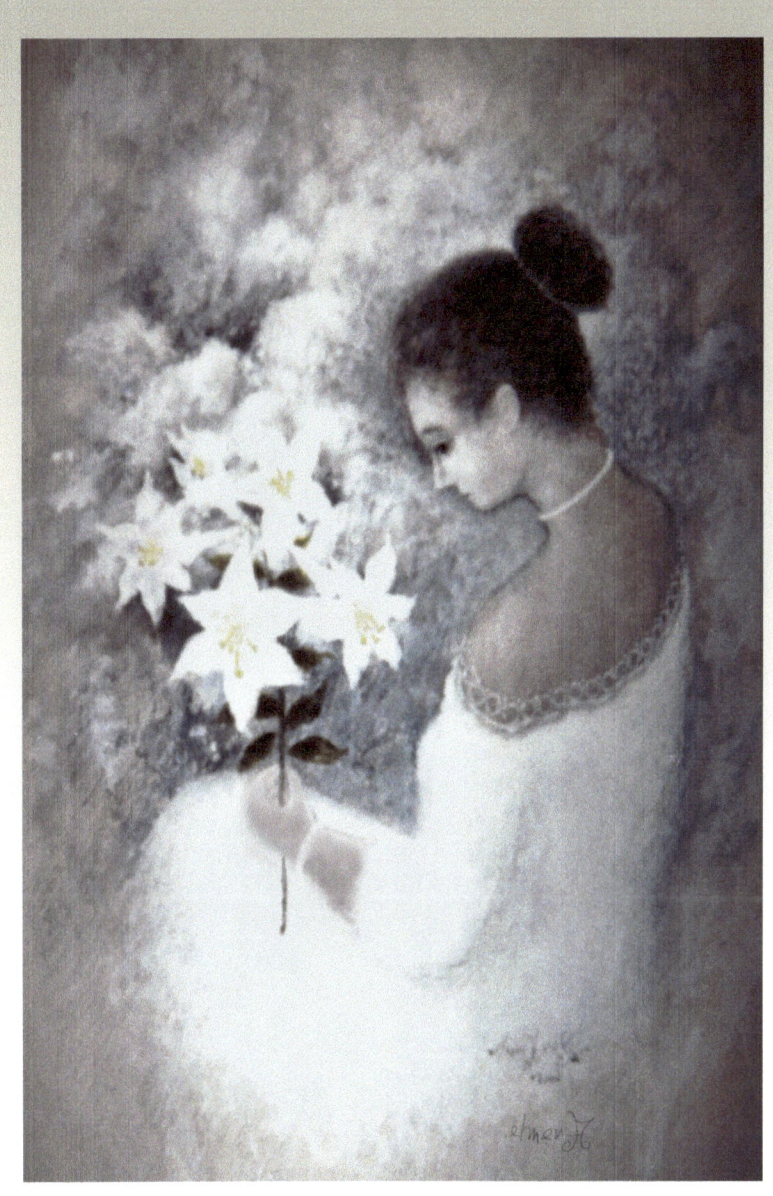

Reflect.
Mixed Media.

28.

*

**Quicker and slicker are not necessarily better.
Speed and skill have little to do with
a profound work of art.**

*

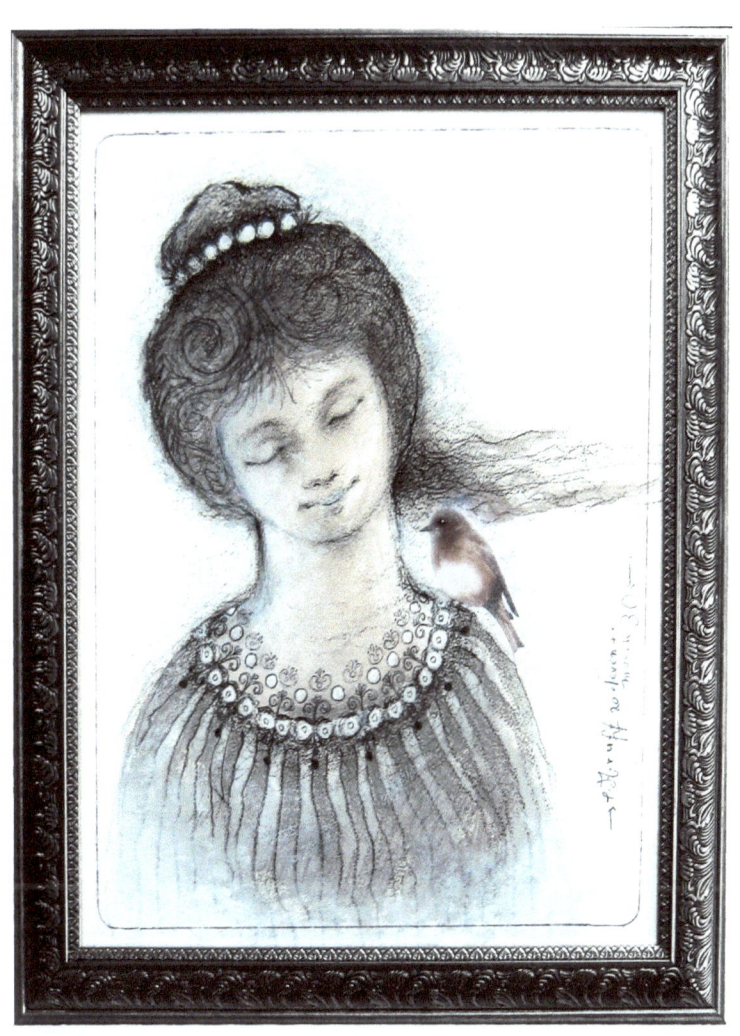

Muse with bird.
Mixed Media.

29.

*

**Always remember that painting
is not a performing art.
It does not require an audience
to watch its creation.
An audience is only necessary when
a painting is complete and exhibited.**

*

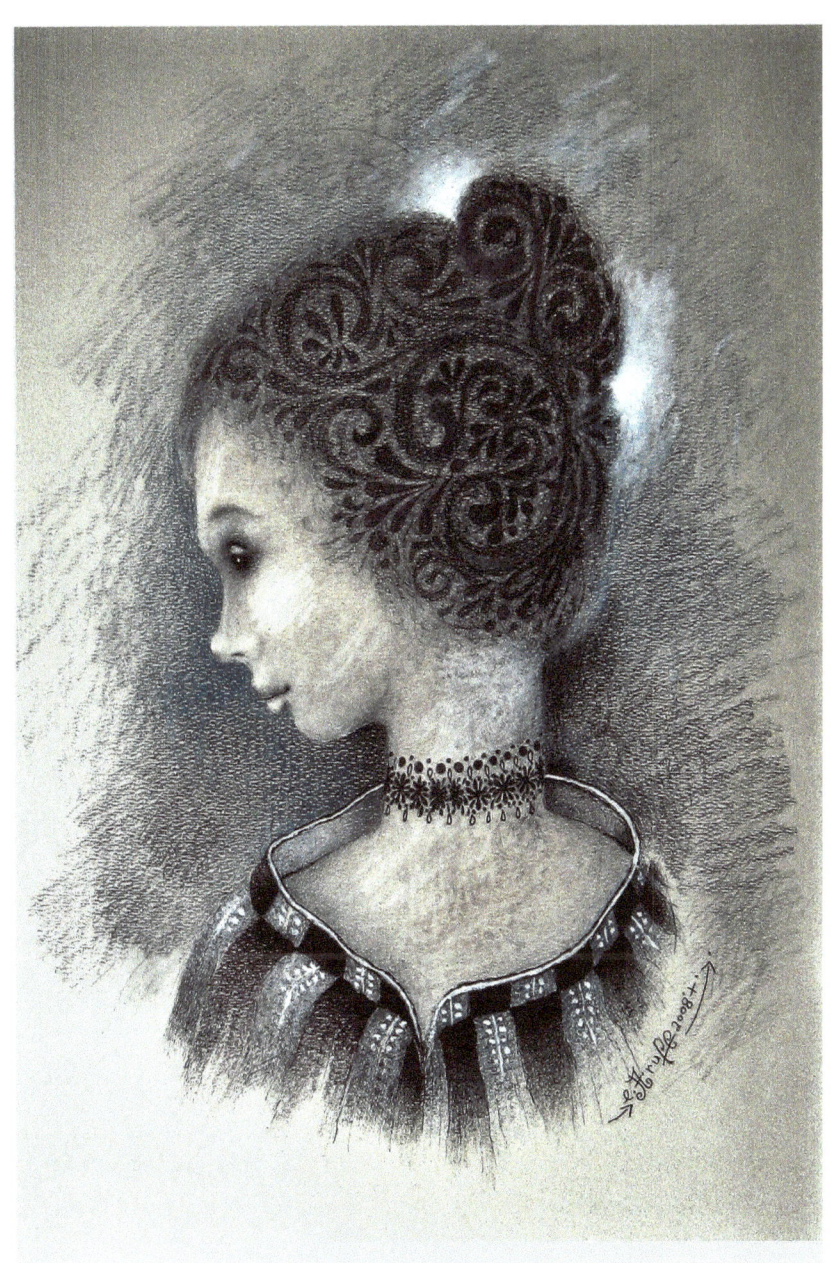

Profile.

Enhanced Print.

30.

*

Unlike all other art forms, paintings are not linear.
Their beginnings, development, and completion
are all given to us at the same time.
Other art forms are linear.
They begin, develop, and conclude in sequence.
Music, literature, dance, theater, and poetry are linear.
They progress from start to finish.
Sculpture is linear in that one must walk
around it in order to appreciate it completely.
*

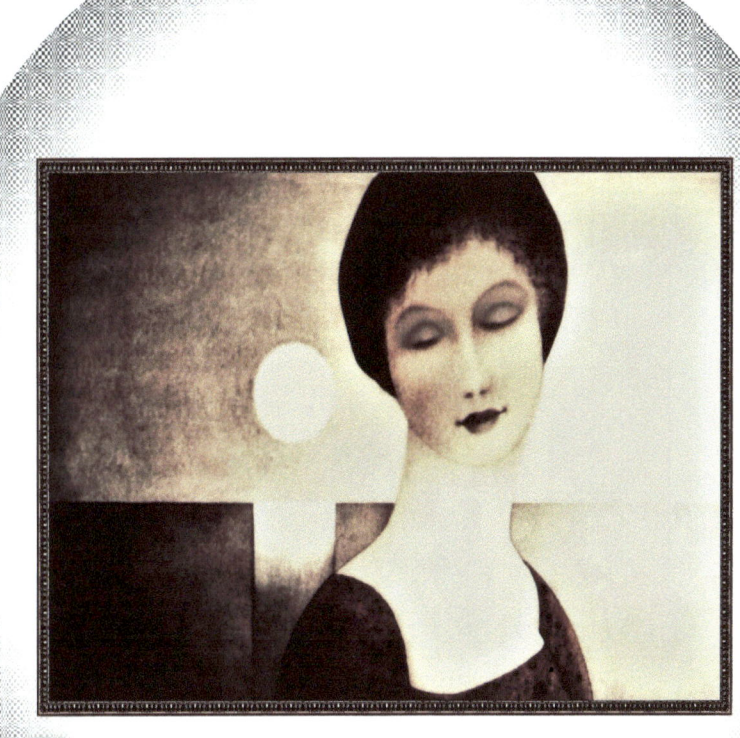

Fantasy.

Watercolor.

31.

*

**If you can tell how a painting was done,
chances are that it is a poor work.
How great paintings are achieved
is always a mystery.**

*

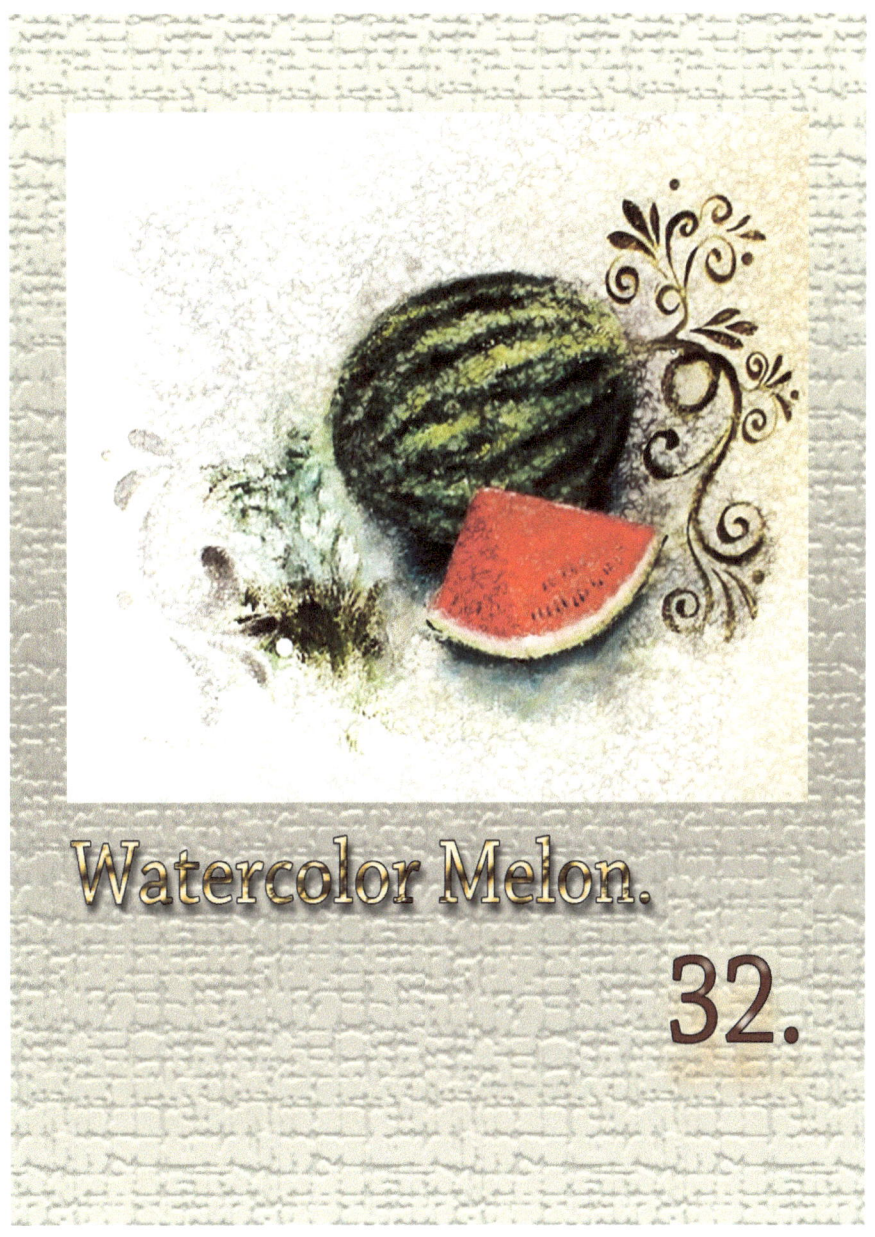

Watercolor Melon.

32.

*

**Continually strive to grow aesthetically;
be critical, and always reach
for what is beyond you.
It is impossible to create beauty that
exceeds our ability to recognize it.
We cannot give more than we have.**

*

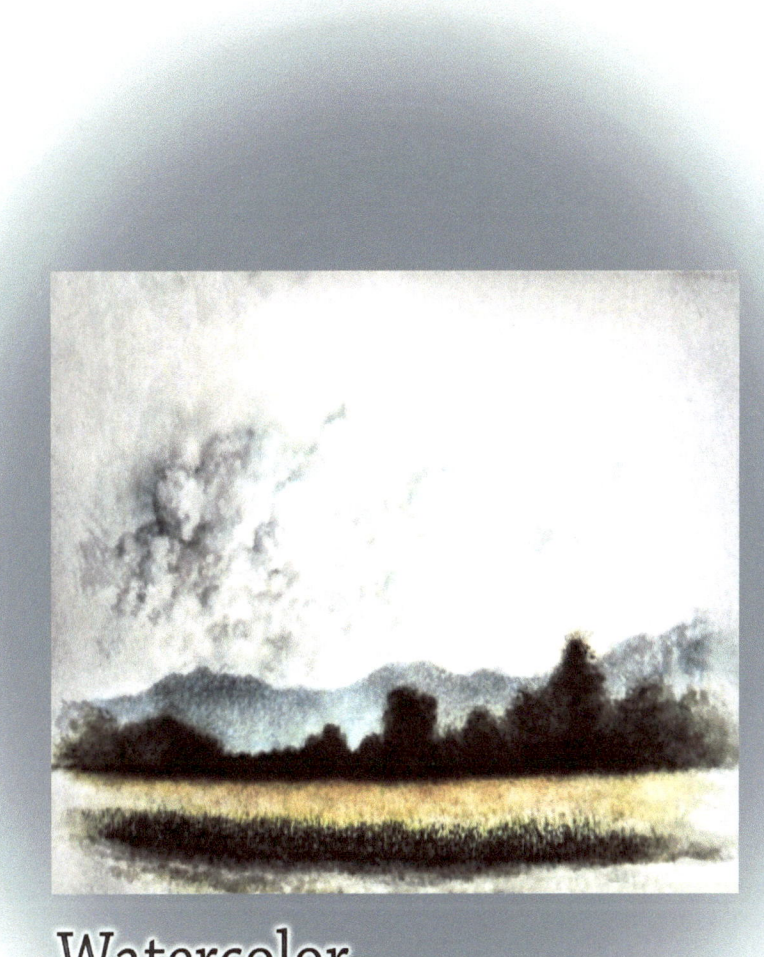

Watercolor.

Shandon.

33.

*

**Do not close your eyes to all that is strange and new.
Fixed and rigid choices are a sure sign of old age.
What is new now often becomes
ordinary with the passage of time...**

*

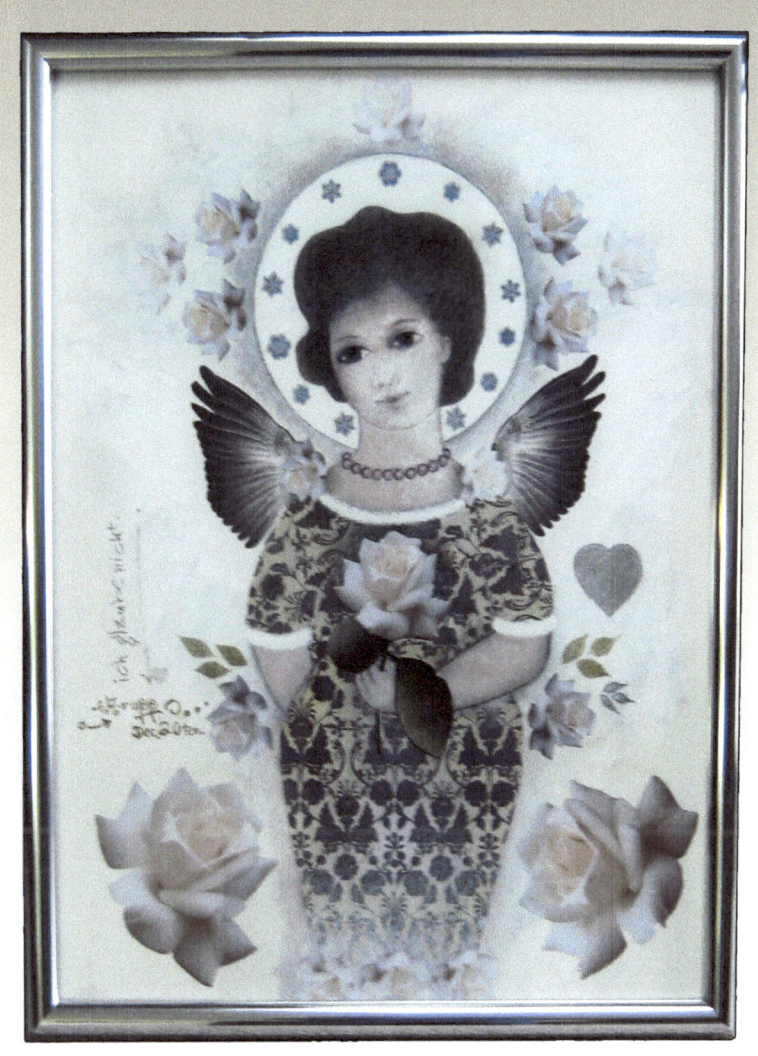

Muse Collage.
Mixed Media.

34.

*

**Form in regard to painting has to do with composition.
The challenge is to create an
entity of the visual elements.
They are hue, value, saturation, texture,
shape, line or edge, and space.**

*

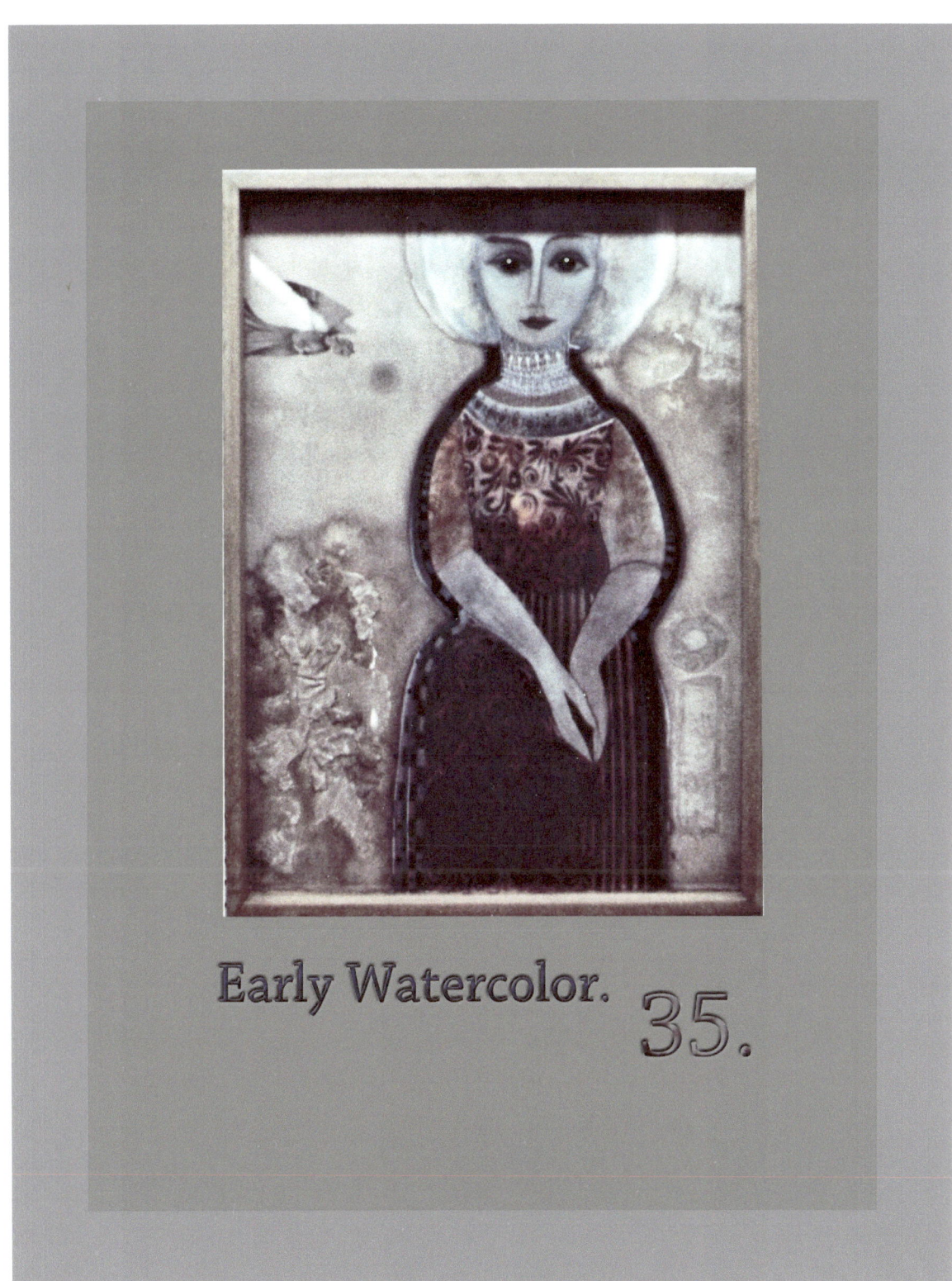

Early Watercolor.

35.

*

**Content refers to the story that a painting tells.
It also refers to subject matter.
Landscape, still life, portrait, and images
in general have to do with the narrative or
iconography of a painting as opposed to
the visual elements of which it is composed.**

*

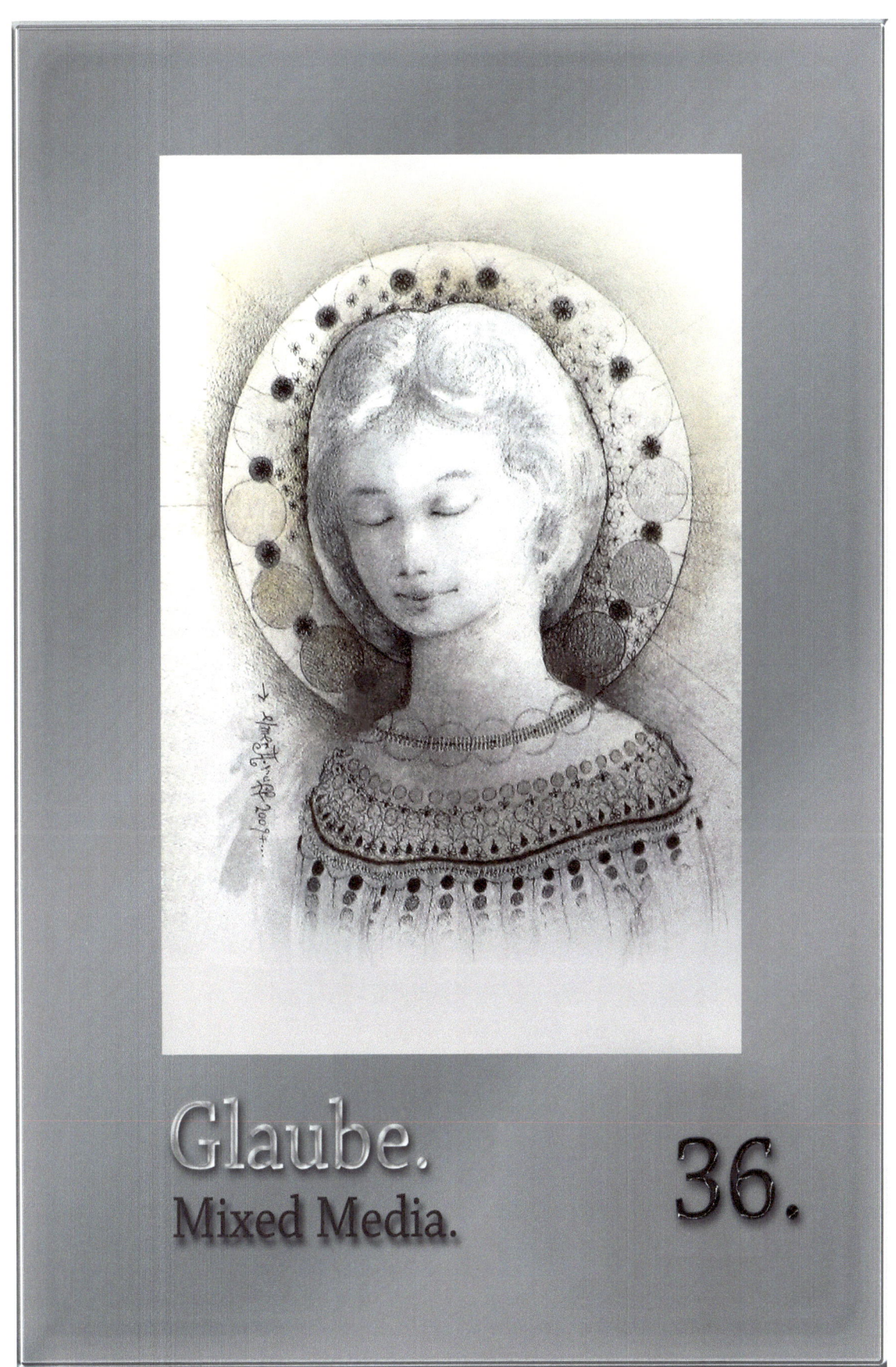

Glaube.
Mixed Media.

36.

*

Content represents the story.
The manner in which it is told is the form.

*

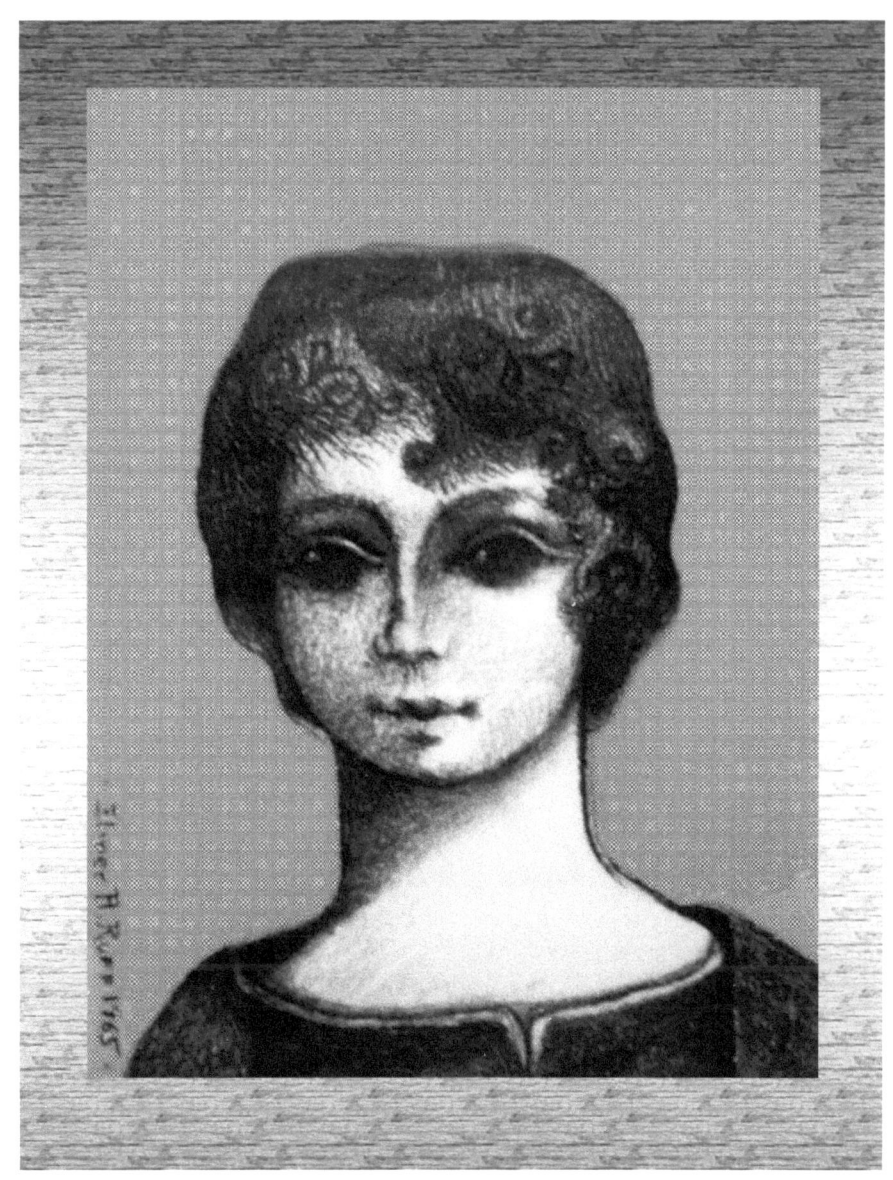

Mixed Media

37.

*

**Content that suggests a history,
as well as describes the present and
suggests what might happen tomorrow,
maximizes its narrative effect.**

*

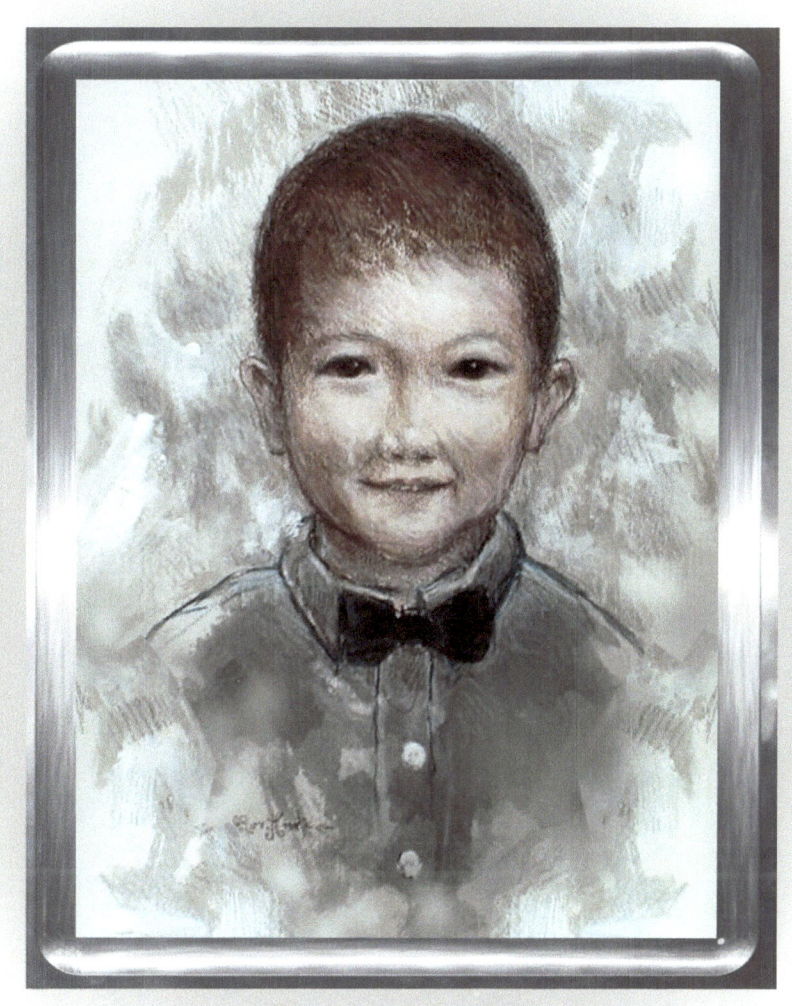

Watercolor Portrait.

38.

*

**Determination without much talent is
better than talent without determination.
If we have both determination and talent,
we are most fortunate.**

*

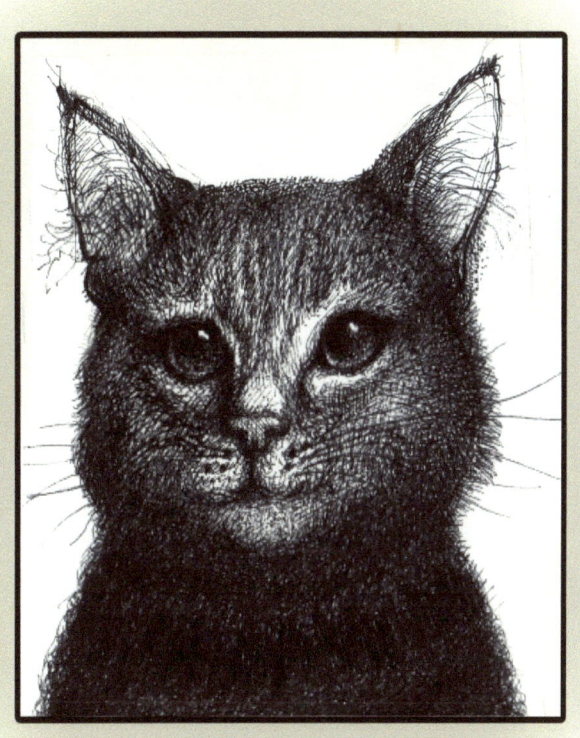

Drawing.

39.

*
Artists are born, not created.
They are right-brained creative personalities.
*

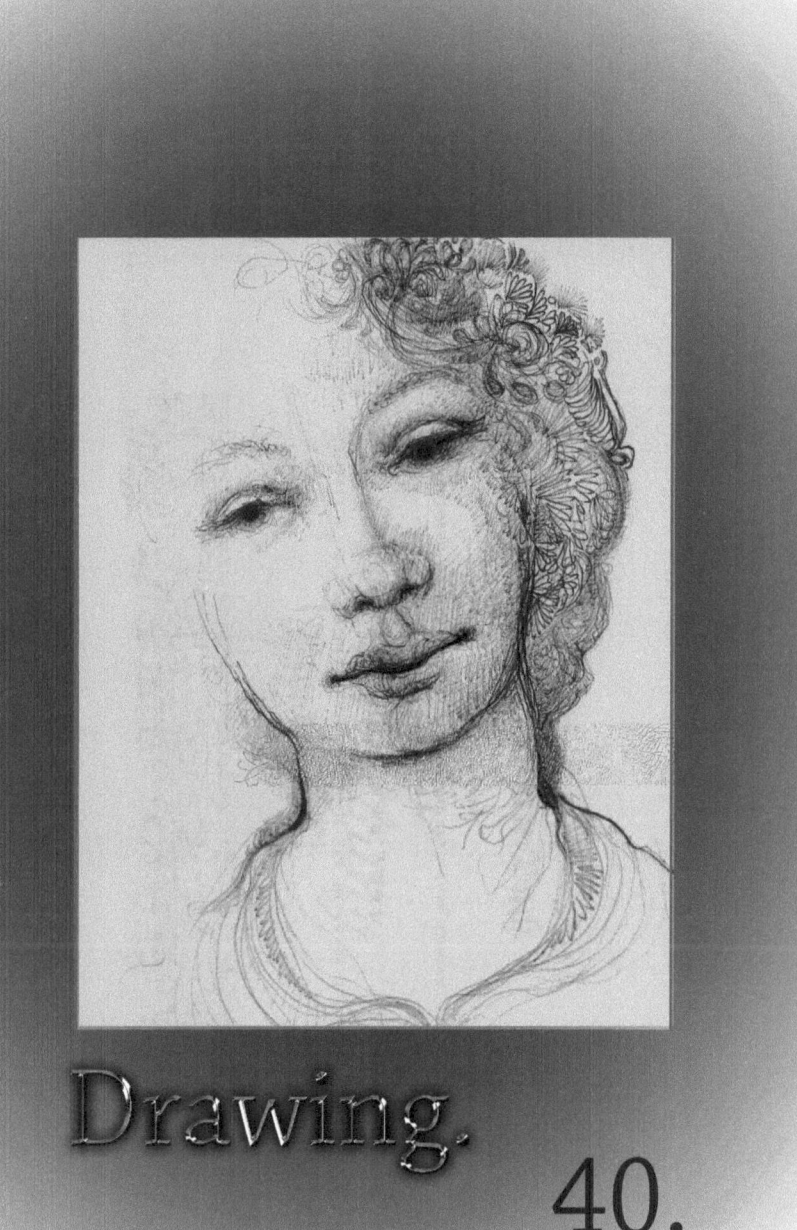

Drawing.

40.

*

Pay as little attention to art critics as possible.
They are all too often self-serving, egocentric
people who seem to enjoy playing God.
I have a brain and vision and am quite capable of
making my own decisions regarding any exhibition.
I do not have to be informed by another person as to
the quality of an exhibit and or any other of its aspects.
I am neither helpless nor stupid!

*

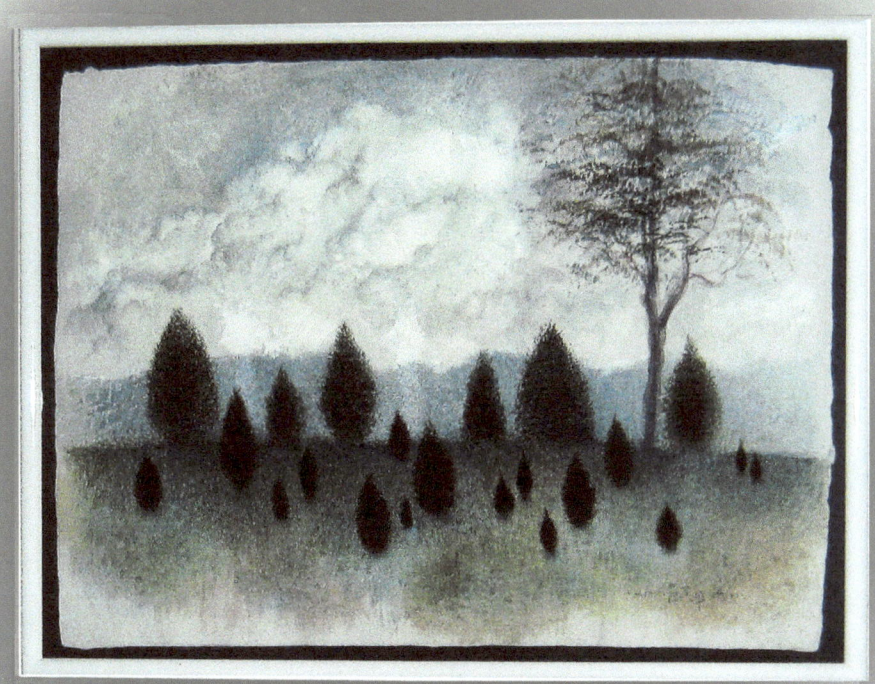

WATERCOLOR   Cedars.

41.

*

**Paintings are composed of parts.
When the parts are put together to form an
absolute unit, the formal aspect of a painting
achieves its maximum formal strength and power.
This includes its aesthetic value.**

*

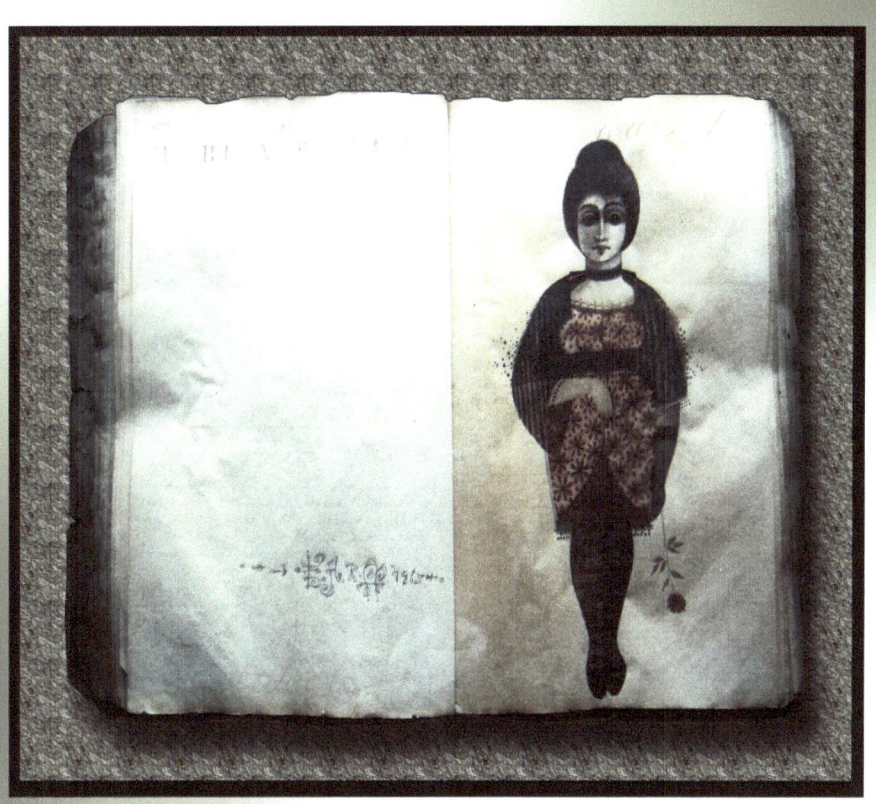

BOOK.
watercolor

42.

*

One of the greatest challenges that a painter has is the achievement of a unity of darks and lights [values]. Perspective and value unity represent the two most common problems students confront in painting.

*

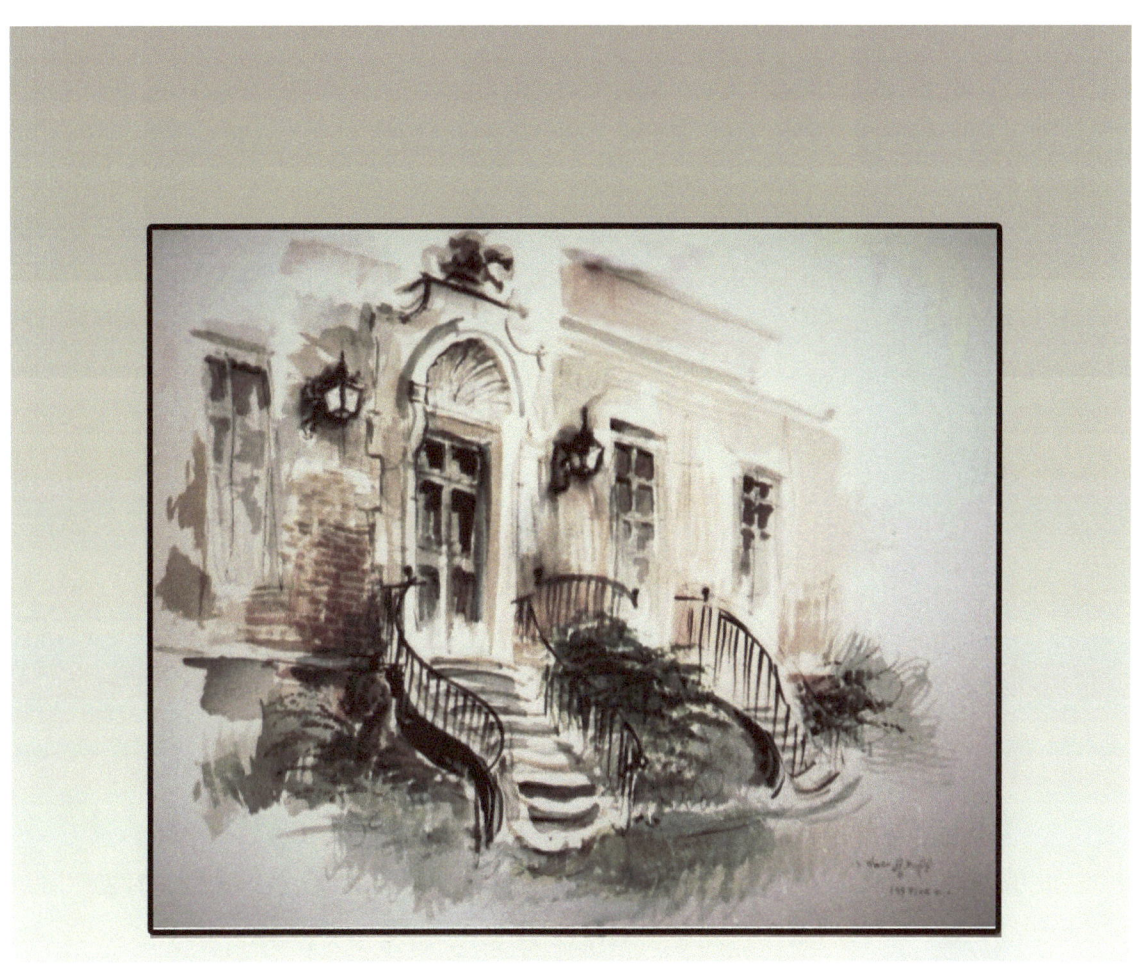

Peterloon.
Watercolor.

43.

*

**Be constantly searching for that
which is explicit in your works.
When explicit visual elements present themselves,
they do so at the expense of the painting's unity.
A painting's parts represent a team and must work
as a team to maximize the work's strength.
We cannot allow any visual element
to upstage the entire painting.
All elements must be a unit.**

*

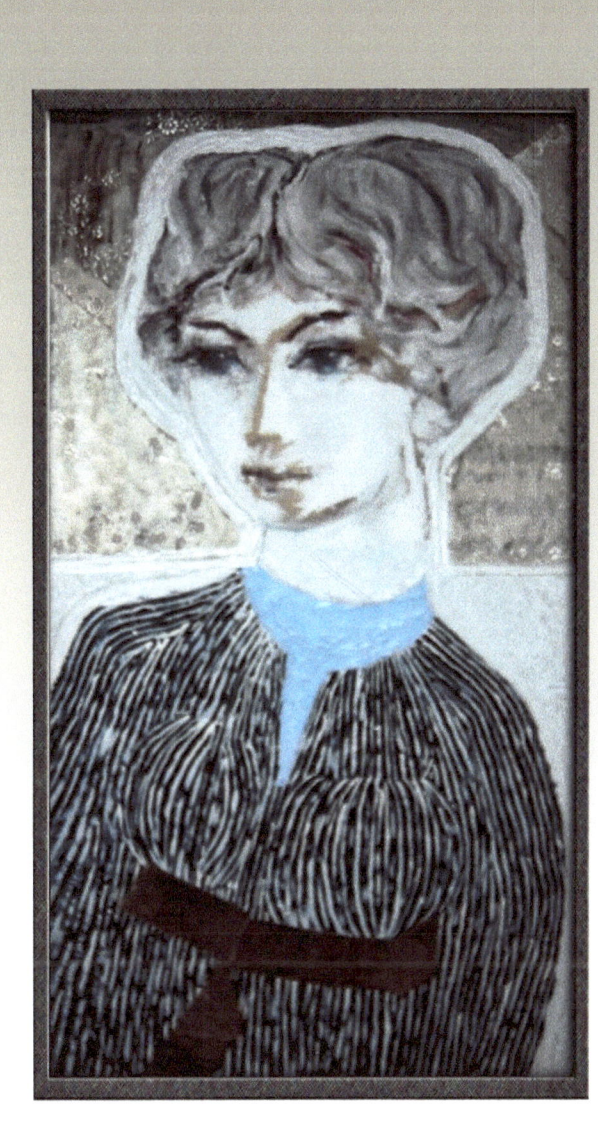

Early Oil. 44.

*

**Have regard and respect for works of art.
Take care of them and store them properly.
Show the same respect and
care for your artist's materials.**

*

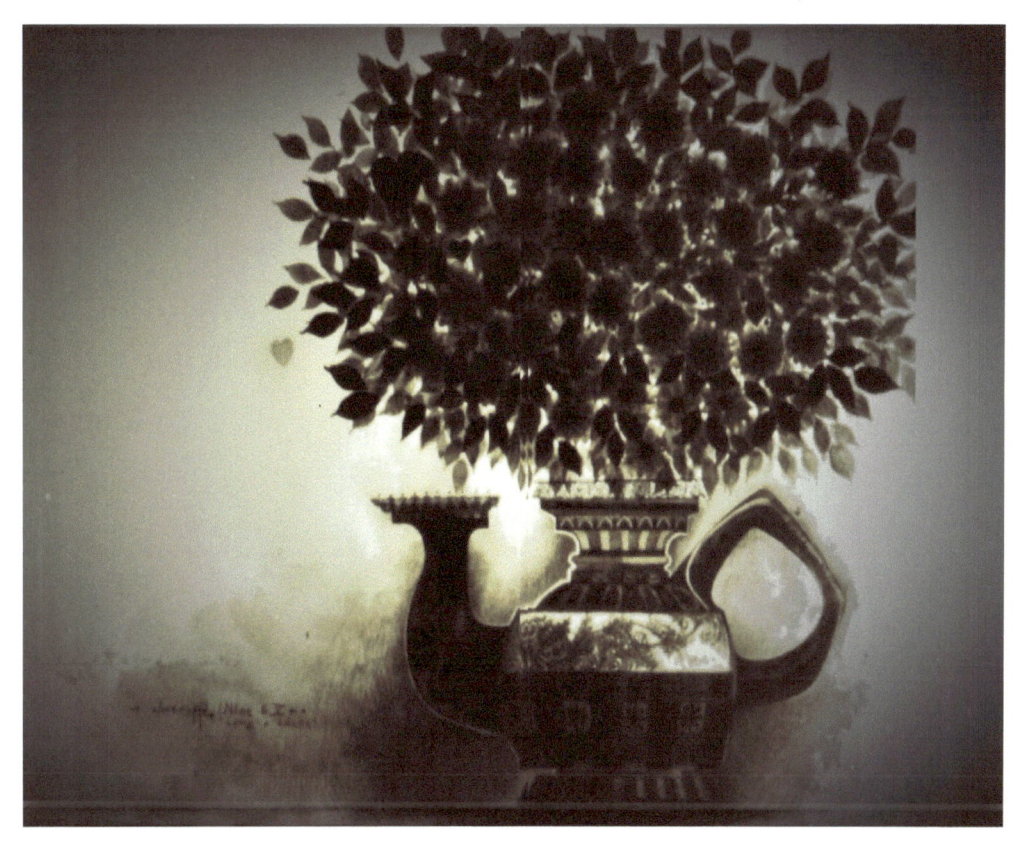

Digital Watercolor.
45.

*

**Never allow your tubes of paint [watercolor, oil, acrylic]
to be stored in places that are excessively cold or hot.
A common mistake is to store them
in the trunk of an automobile.**

*

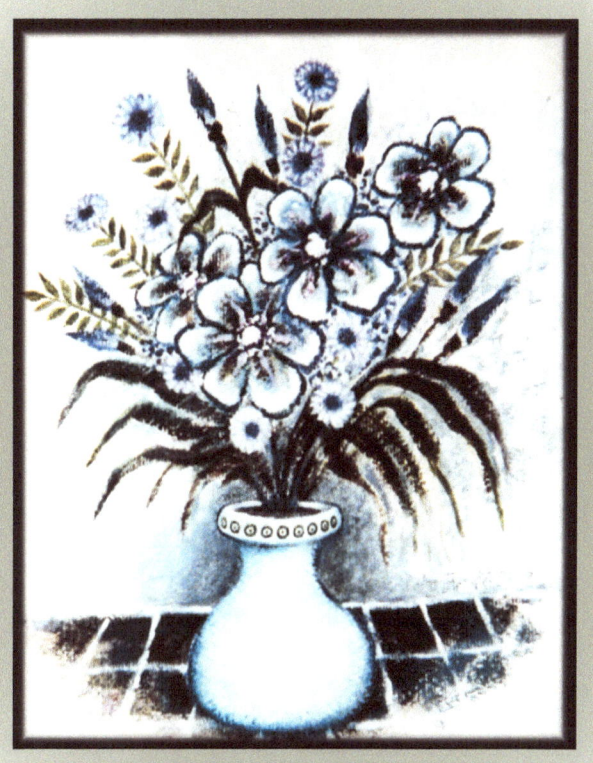

Acrylic.

46.

*

Keep a good supply of new ideas for future works.
Make notes, make sketches, collect
visual images, photographs, etc.
Review your collection of ideas from time to time.
Incentive regarding a particular idea can become stale.

*

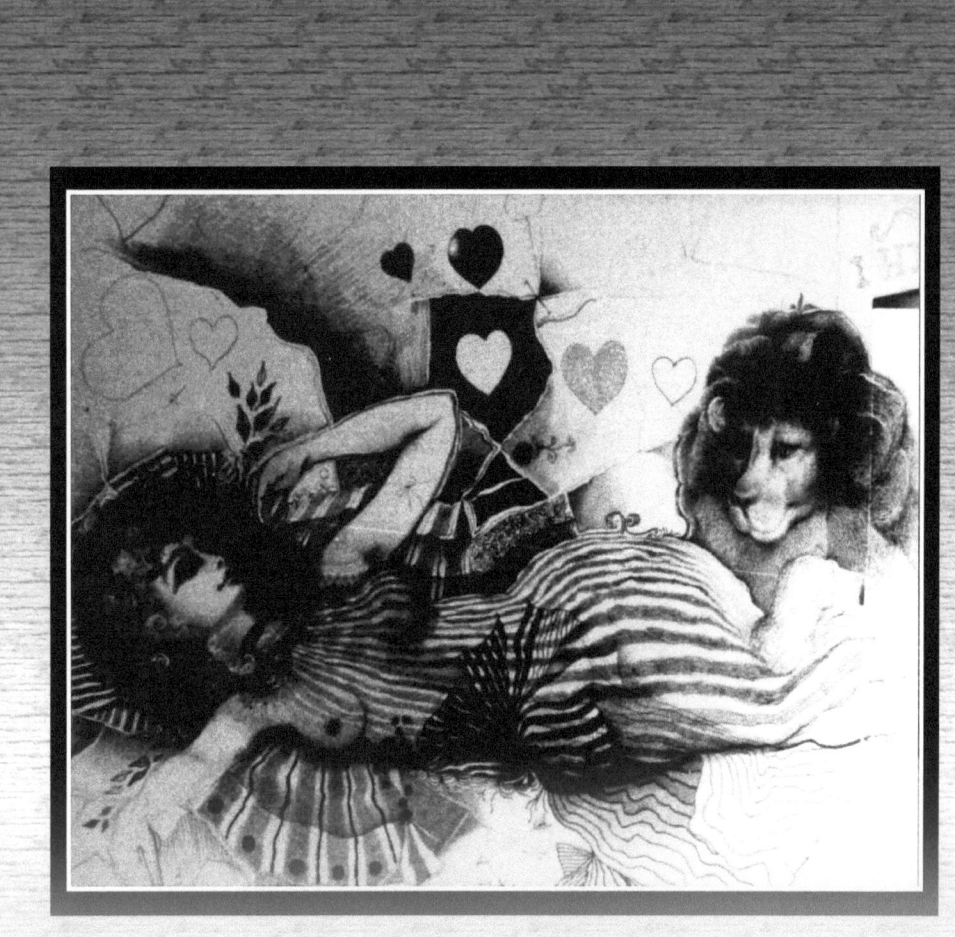

Mixed Media.

47.

*

**Learn the language of art.
Know the meaning of its terms
and their proper pronunciation.
Each discipline has its unique idioms.**

*

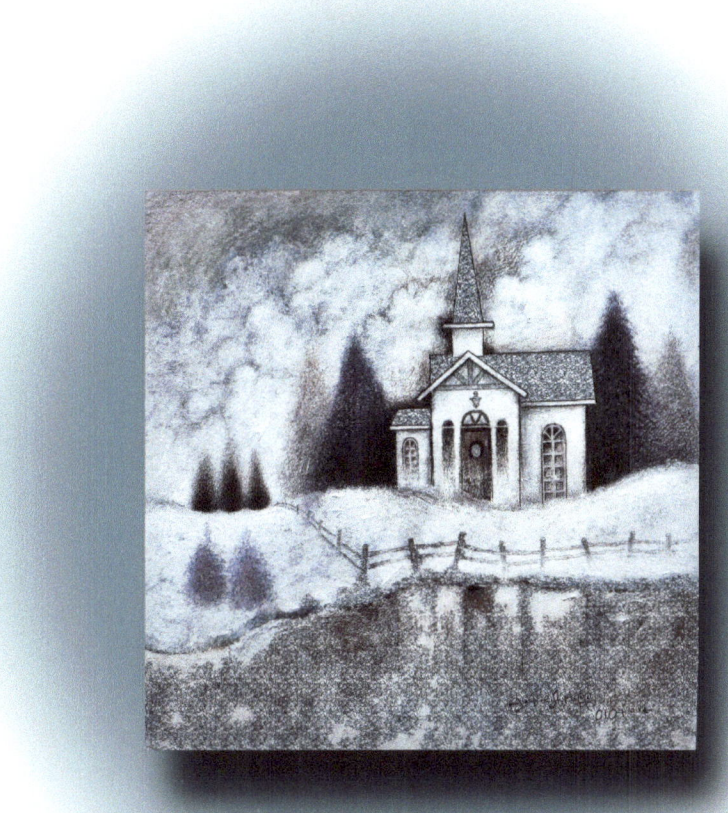

Mixed Media.

48.

*

**Attend classes regularly.
Arrive early, and try to
make up missed classes.**

*

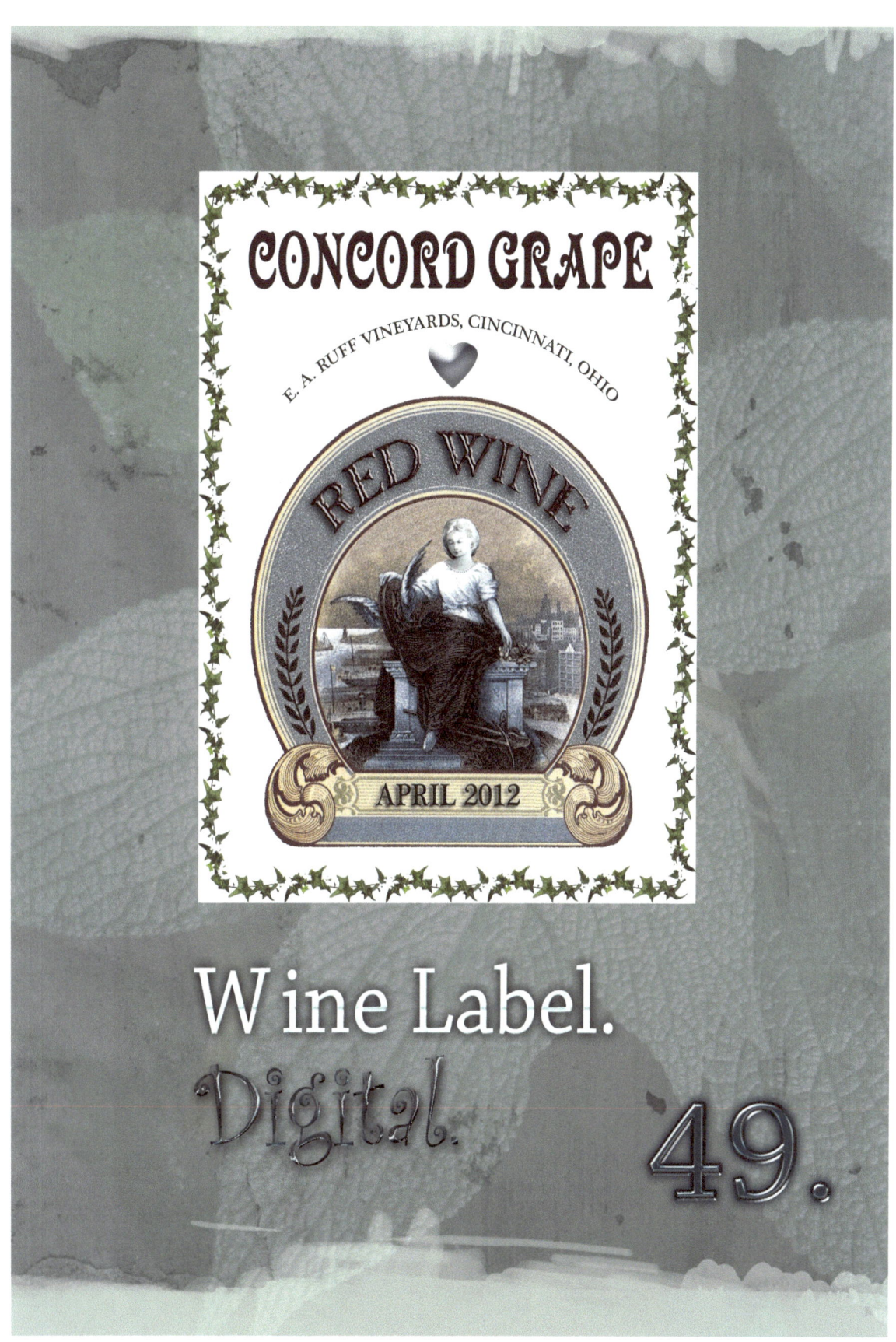

Wine Label.

Digital.

49.

*

**It is wise to keep an art notebook.
It should contain sketches,
clippings, noted ideas, formulas,
personal thoughts, etc.**

*

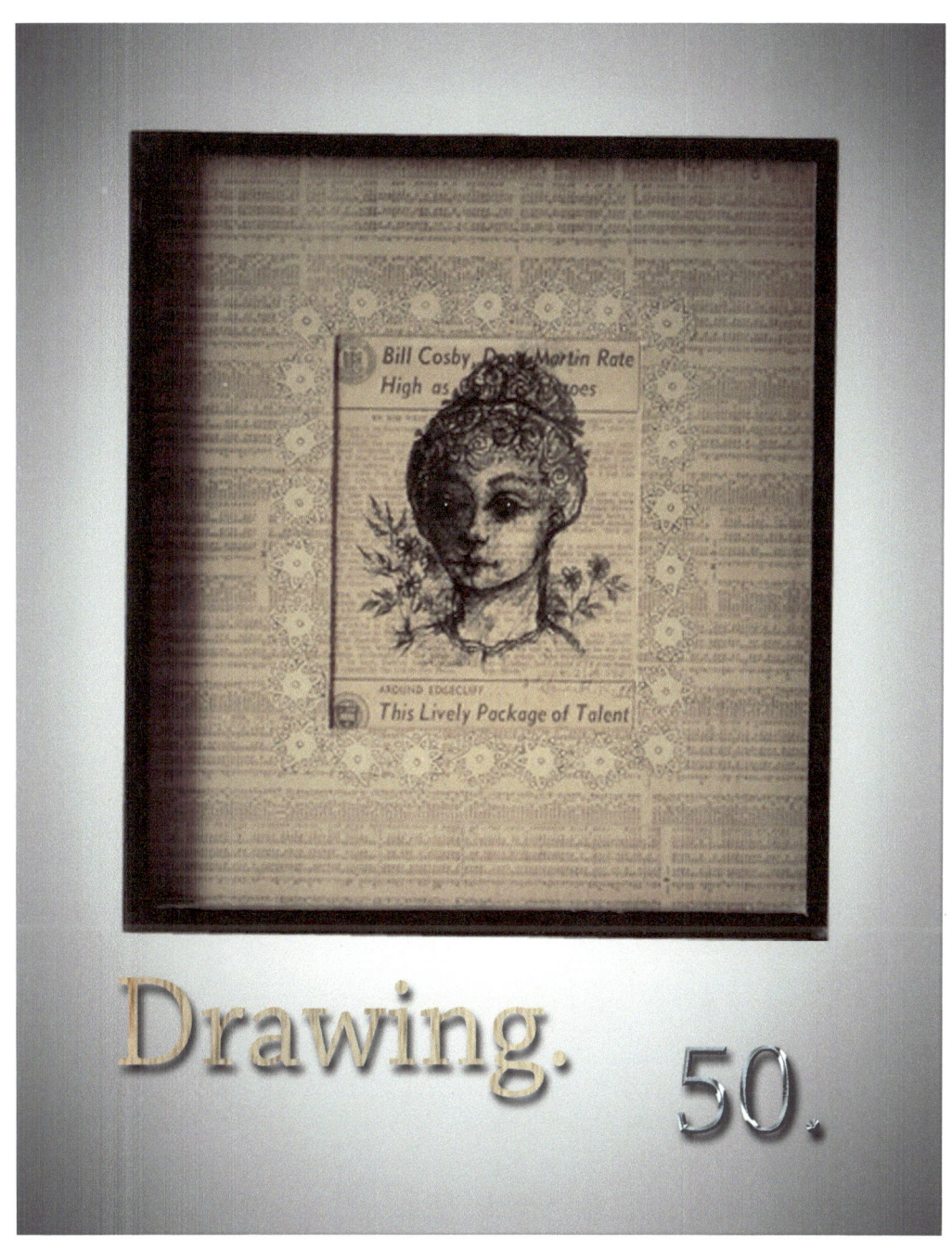

Drawing.

50.

*

**Make notes of those things of interest
that may arise during the class session,
and include them in your notebook.**

*

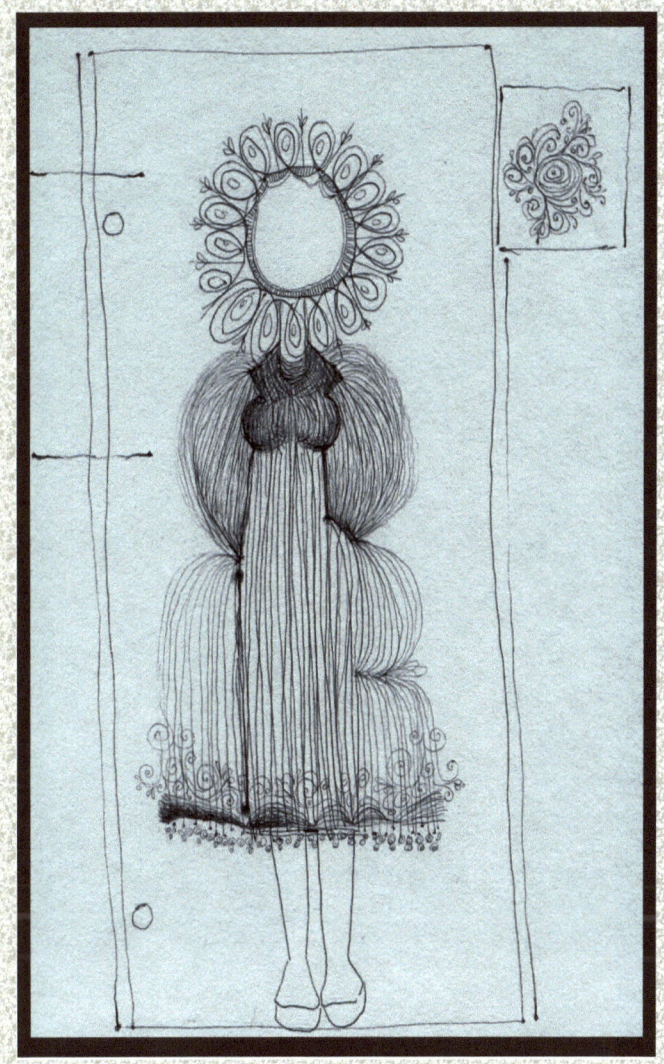

Early Drawing

51.

*

It is wise to step away from your work from
time to time in order to see it better.
Other methods of achieving a visual
evaluation of your work include viewing the
work in a mirror, using a reducing glass,
placing it where you can see it every day,
or putting it out of sight for a while.

*

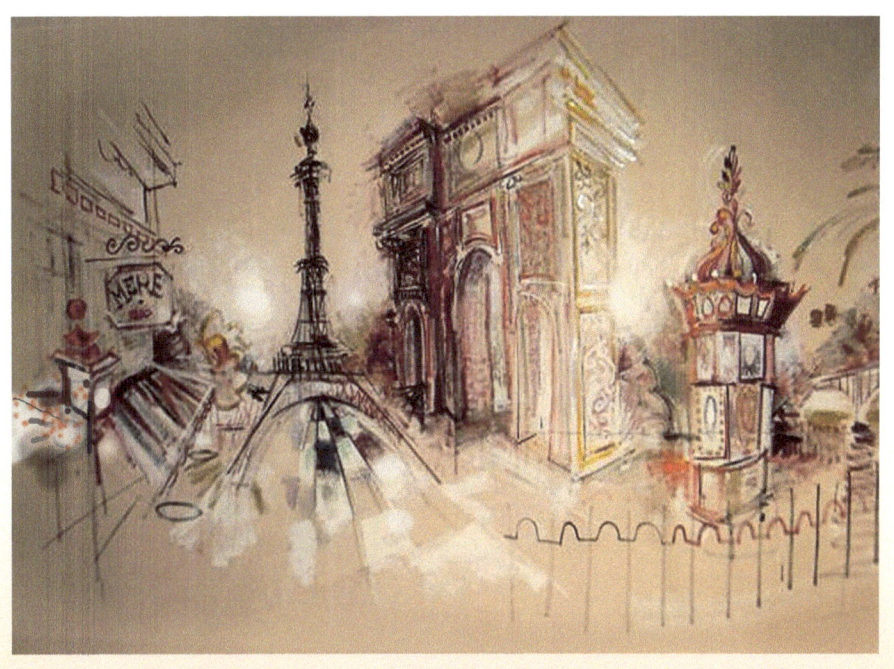

Mural Fragment.

52.

*

**During class, it is wise to take time out and
walk about to see what others are doing.
Once an hour is recommended.**

*

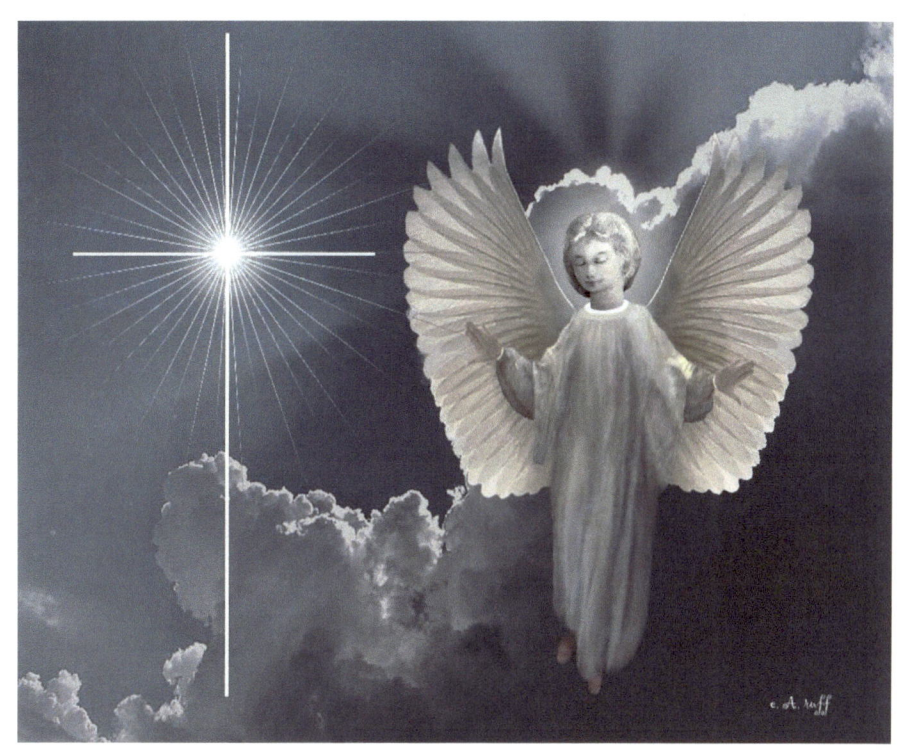

Digital Collage.

53.

*

Avoid special effects and gimmicks like wet into wet, salt, sponges, credit cards, splattering, special brushes, etc.

*

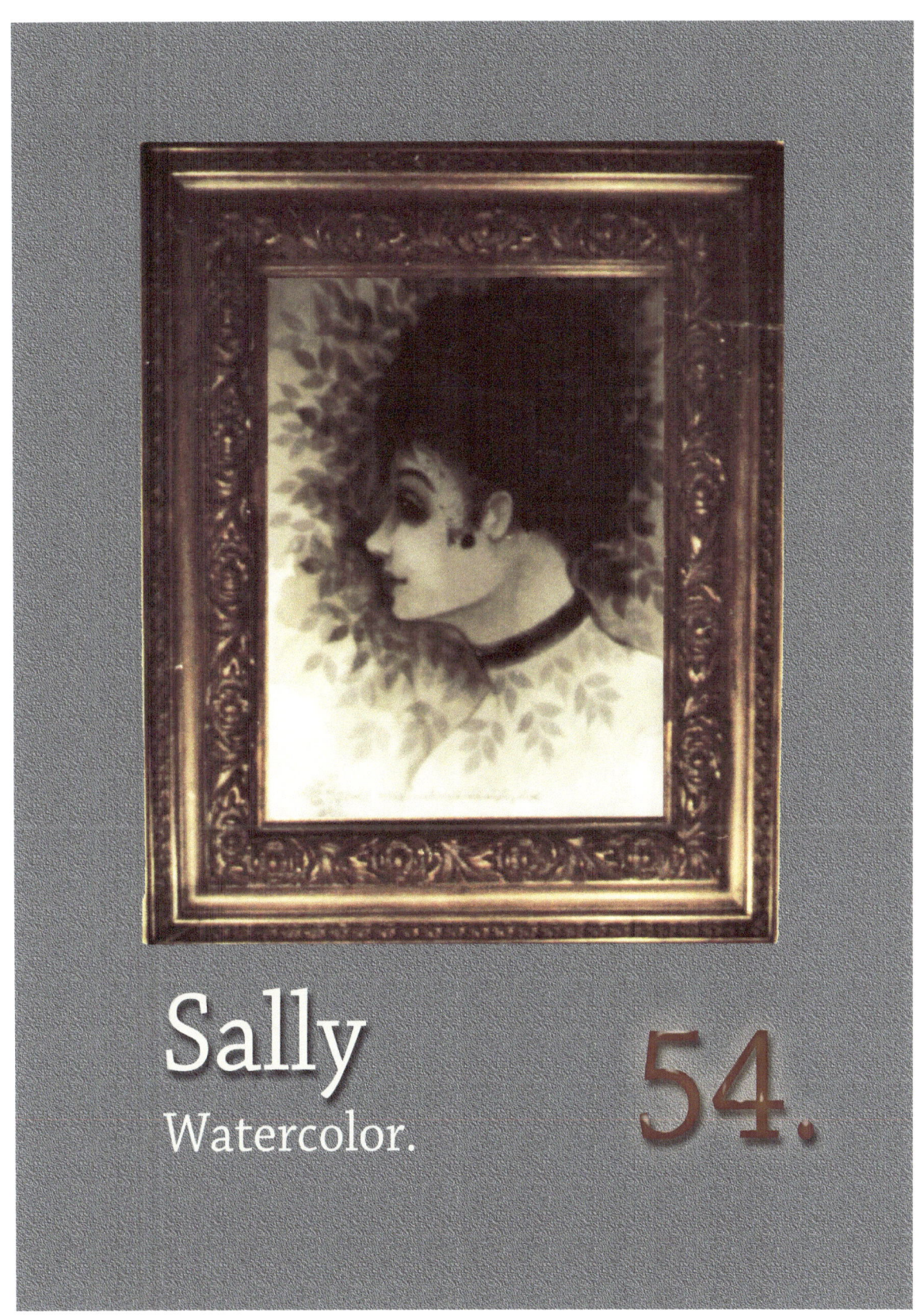

Sally
Watercolor.

54.

*

**A fine painting combines three ingredients:
the personality of the artist, the personality of
the subject, and the personality of the medium.**

*

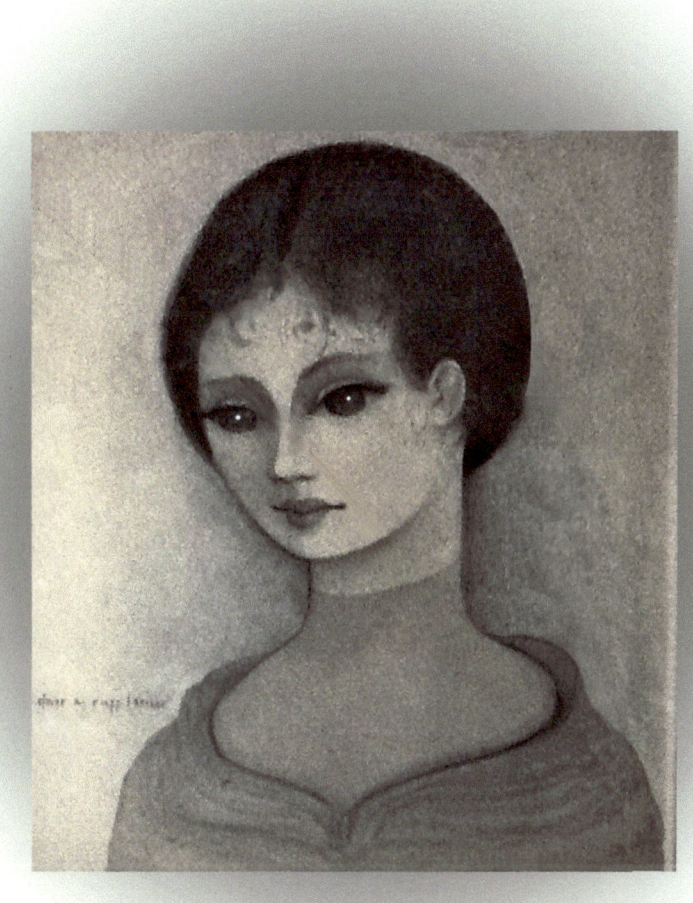

She.
Watercolor.

55.

*

Try to avoid buying methods books that are not generic. Avoid books written and illustrated by artists teaching only their own method or style of painting.

*

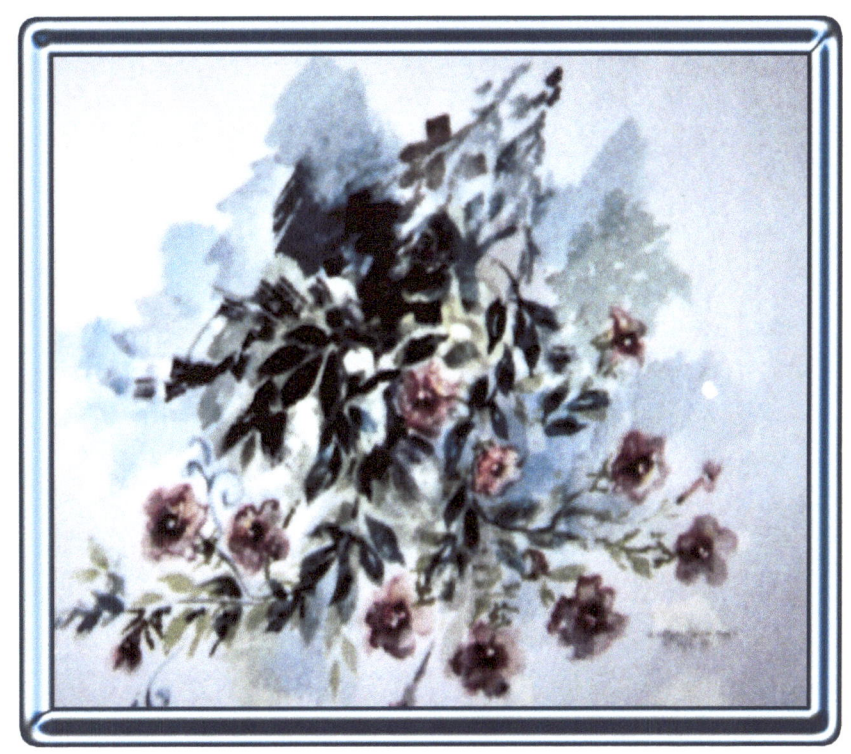

Watercolor.

56.

*

**It is always wise to do several thumbnail
sketches prior to starting a new work.**

*

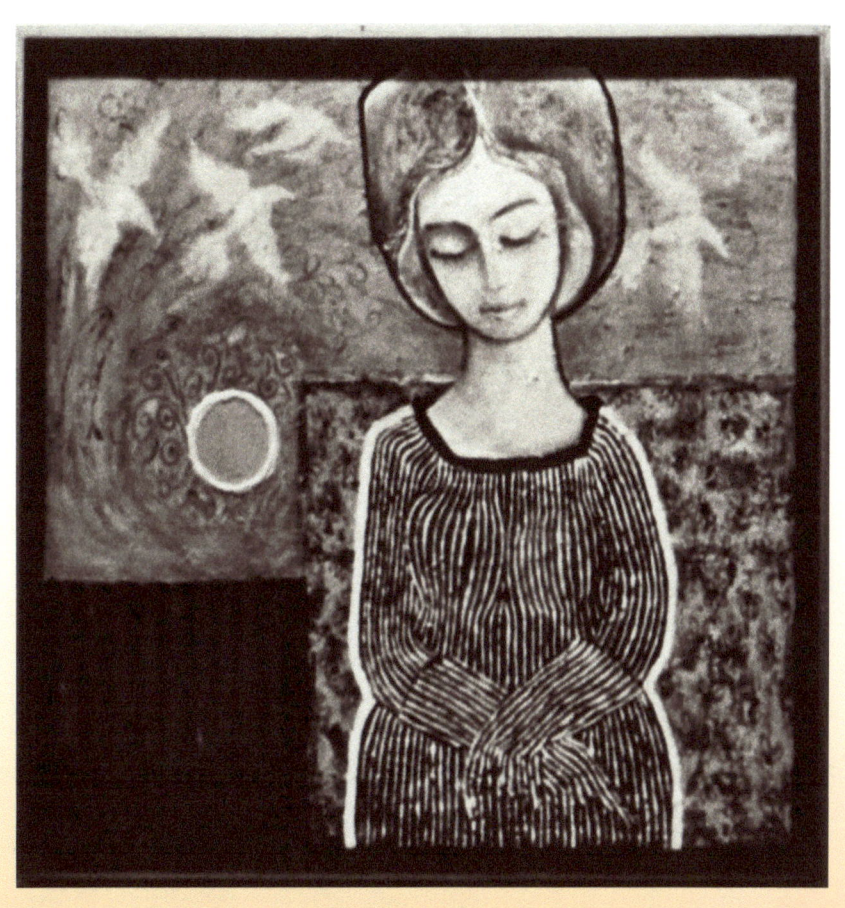

Early Oil.

57.

*

If you don't understand something in class, ask to have it explained until you do understand it.

*

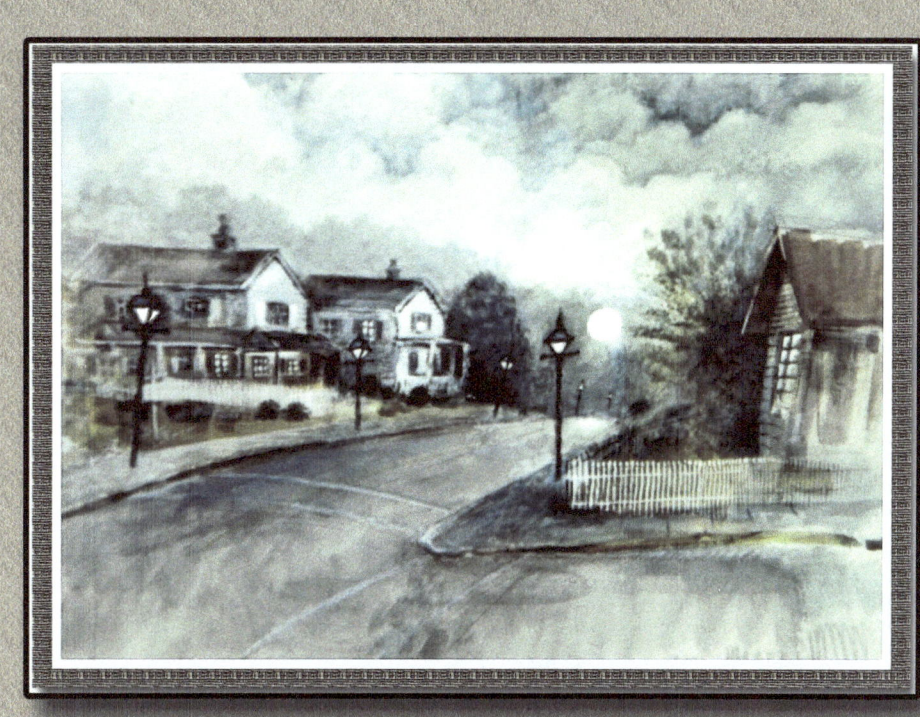

Watercolor.

58.

*

It is perfectly fine to paint over an old oil painting, providing it is not crazed and/or impasto. Impasto means thick paint. The word is Italian.

*

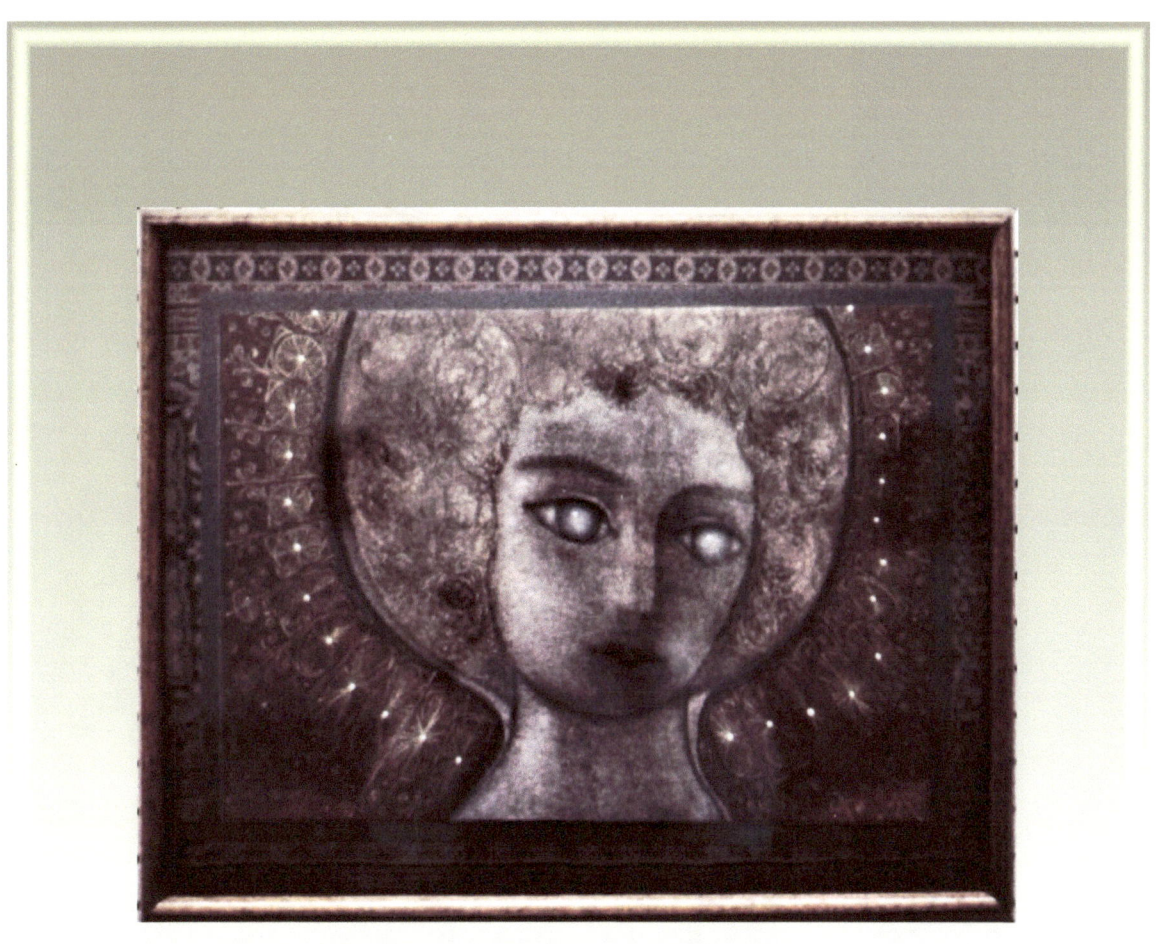

Blind girl.

59.

*

Rules for changing media:
It is acceptable to paint oil over acrylic.
It is not acceptable to paint acrylic over oil.
It is acceptable to paint oil over casein.

*

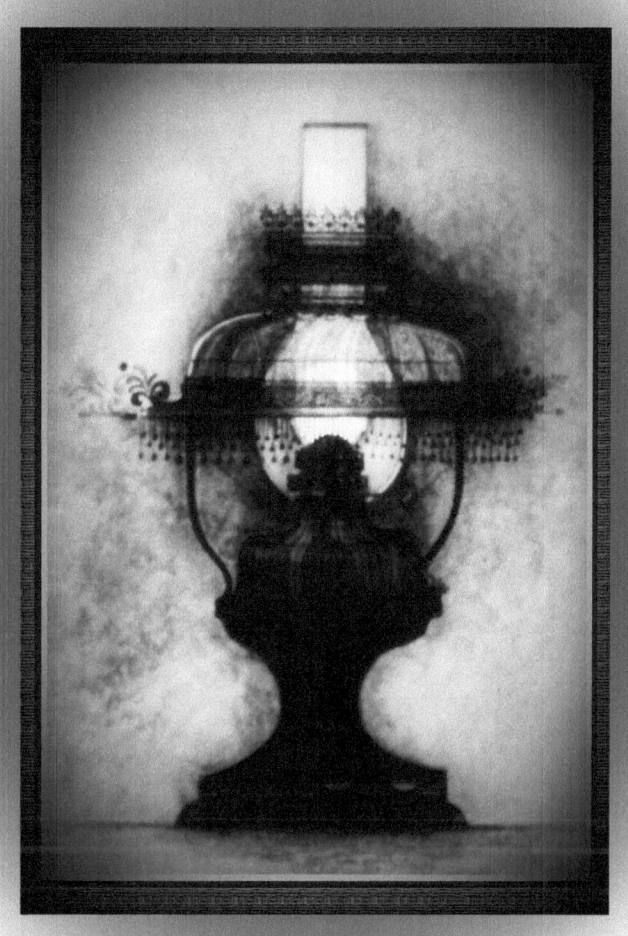

Watercolor.

*

**Many great works of art are metaphorical
and speak to us on two or more levels.
In addition, it is not unusual for a great
work of art to be autobiographical.**

*

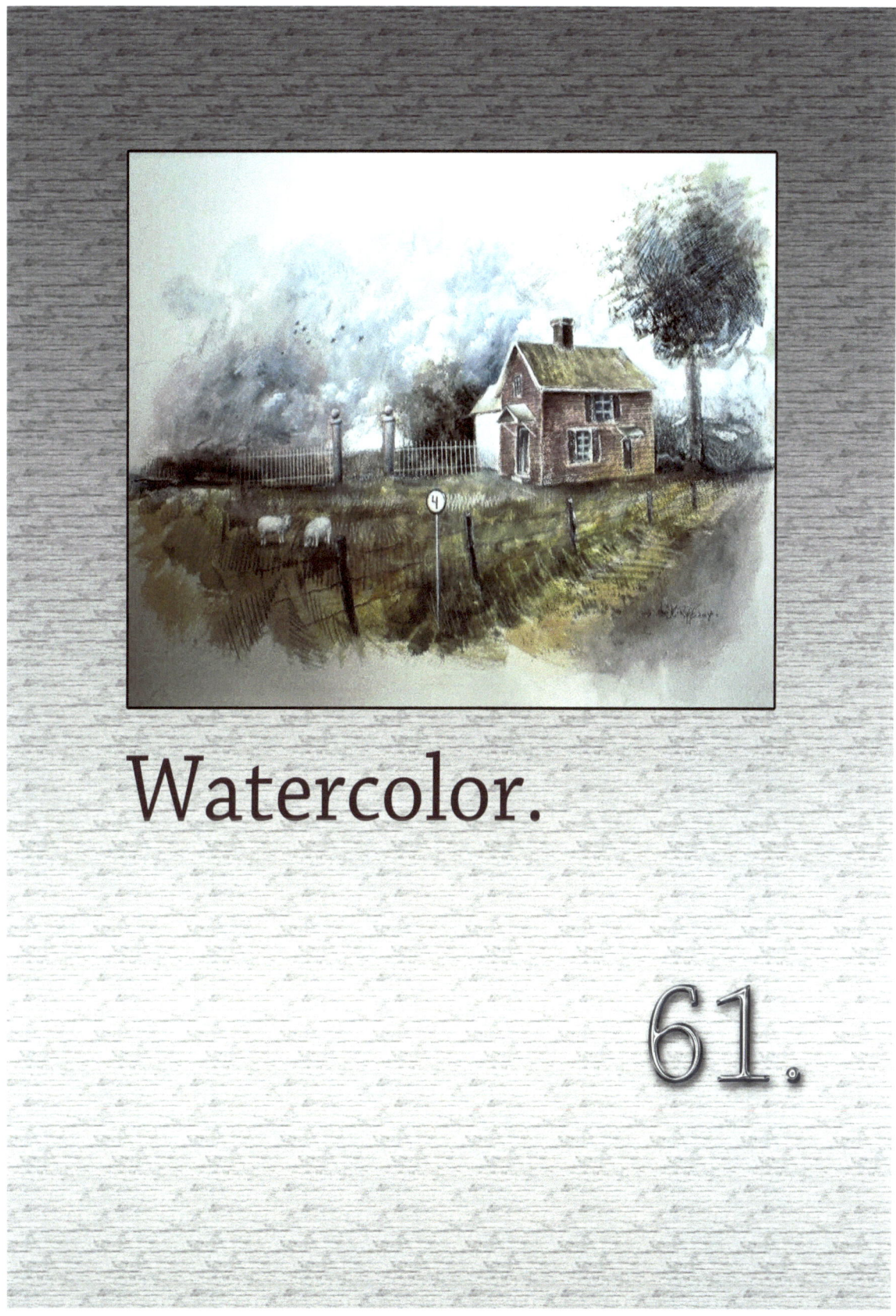

Watercolor.

61.

*

**Achieving the status of qualifying to be included
in art history texts involves fifty percent
ability and fifty percent mythology.
Greatness is usually exaggerated.
There are now and have been in the past many
persons qualifying for greatness who were
never recognized as such simply because they
lacked the myth of recognized greatness.**

*

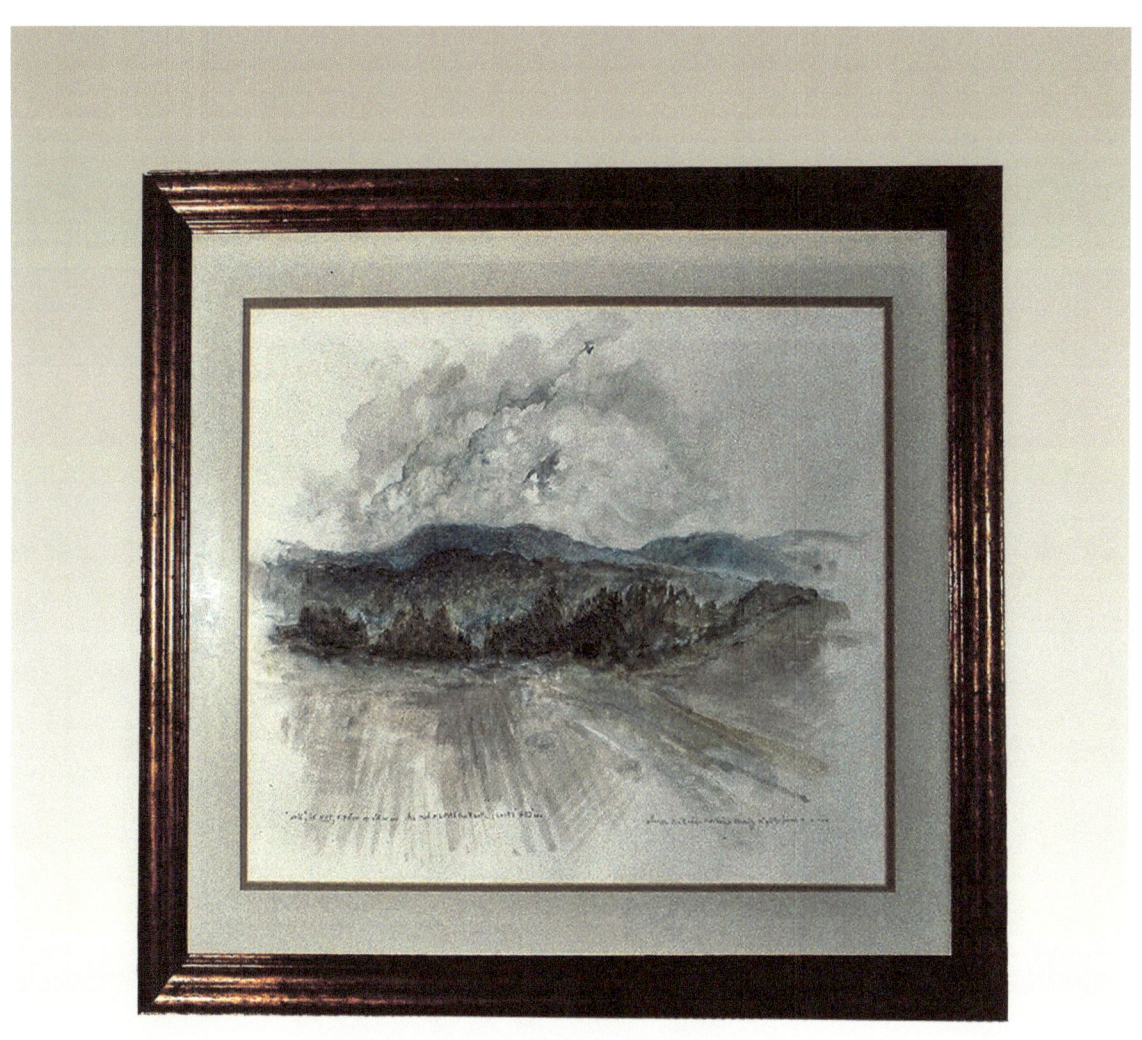

Watercolor.

62.

*

Large problems in a given painting always mask smaller problems.

*

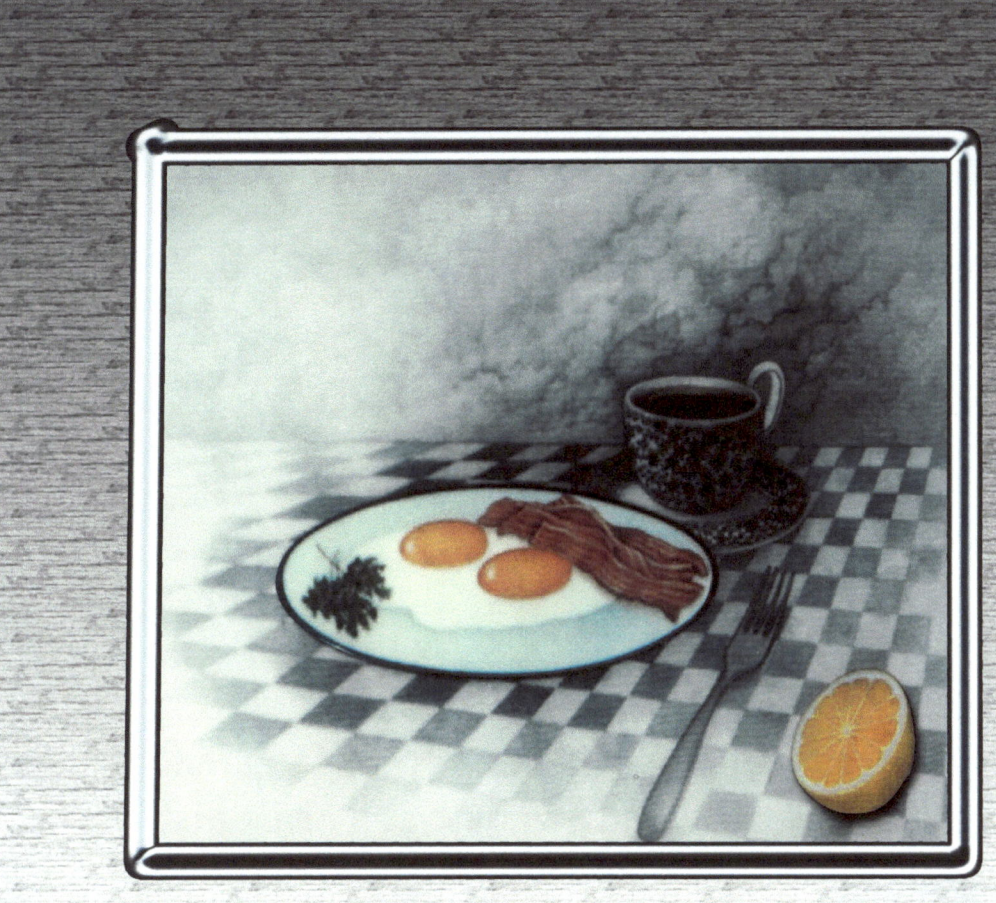

Breakfast.

63.

*

**Paintings seem to have an effective focal length;
that is to say, they function best at a given distance.
This is something that the artist can determine.**

*

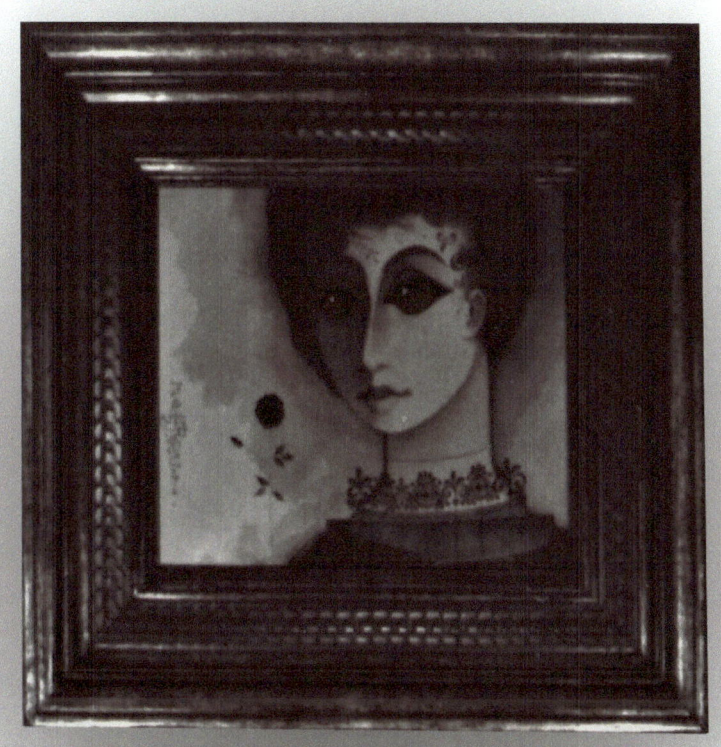

Watercolor.

64.

*

**Ideally, a painting should be viewed
in the same light circumstances
in which the artist painted it.
This is not always possible.**

*

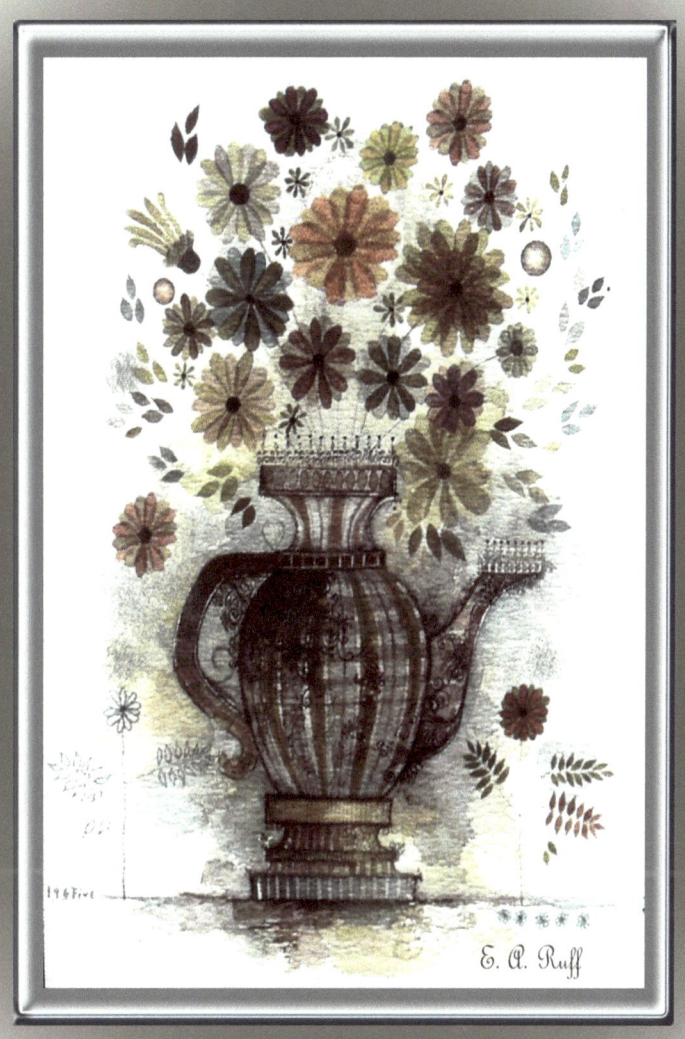

Watercolor.

65.

*

**Most art instructors place little
emphasis upon brush preparation.
Much success in applying paint depends upon
the manner in which the brush has been prepared.
Consideration has to be given to such things as
color mixing, viscosity, quantity, pigmentation,
brush style, bristles, pressure, angle, etc.**

*

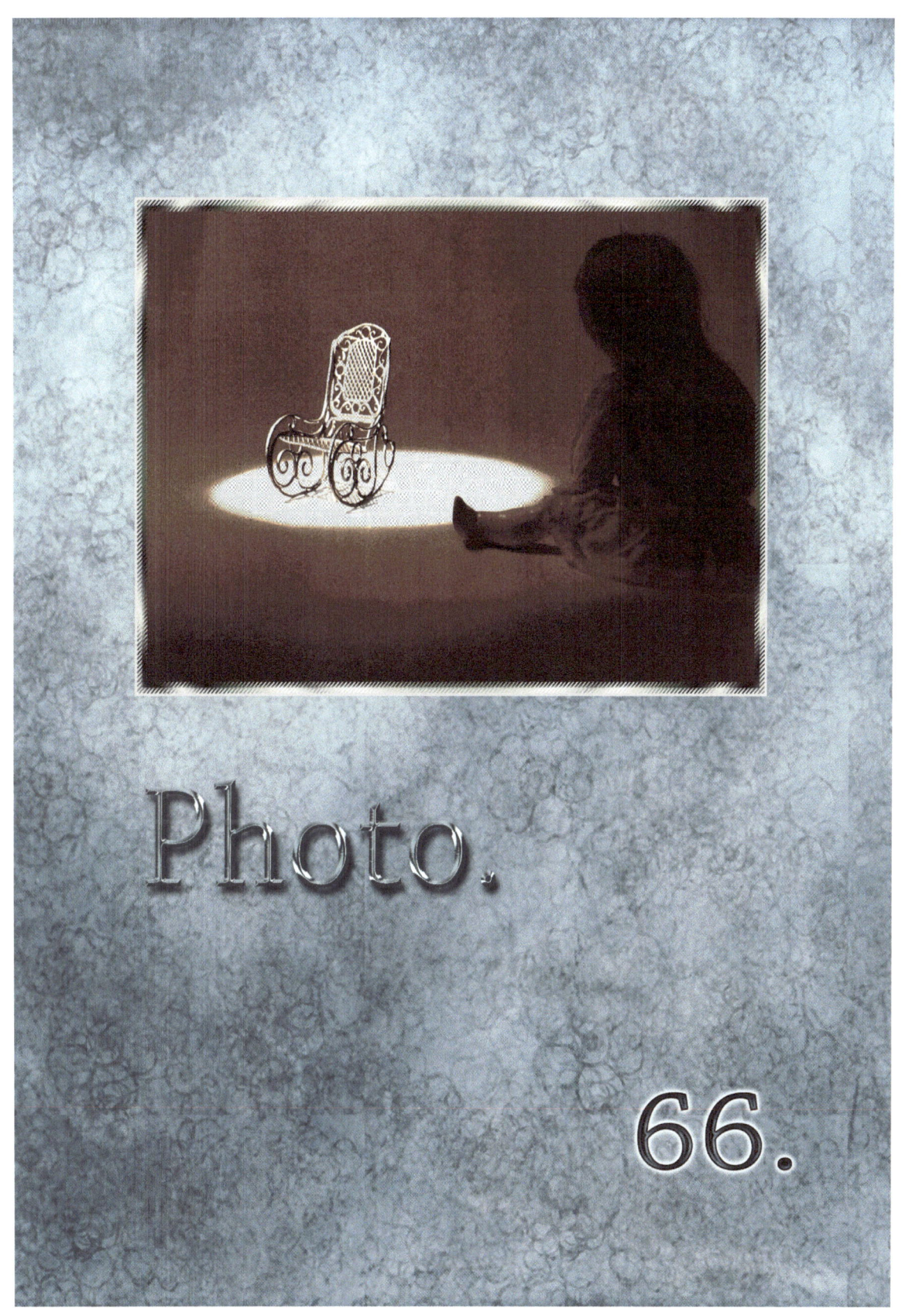

Photo.

66.

*

No matter what the medium,
the pigments in it are the same.
It is the vehicle that determines
what a medium is called.
The vehicle is the glue that binds
the pigments to the surface.
Three basic binders are linseed oil,
acrylic polymer, and gum tragacanth.

*

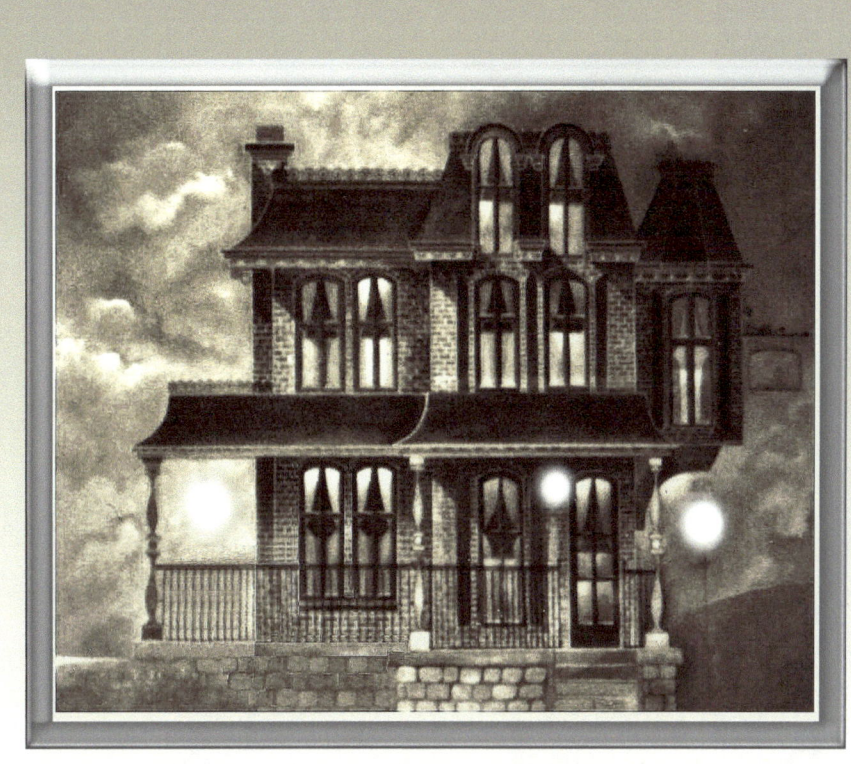

Watercolor.

67.

*

Just as we intone words to give them additional meaning,
it is possible to intone brush strokes.
There are angry brush strokes, loving brush
strokes, timid brush strokes, etc.

*

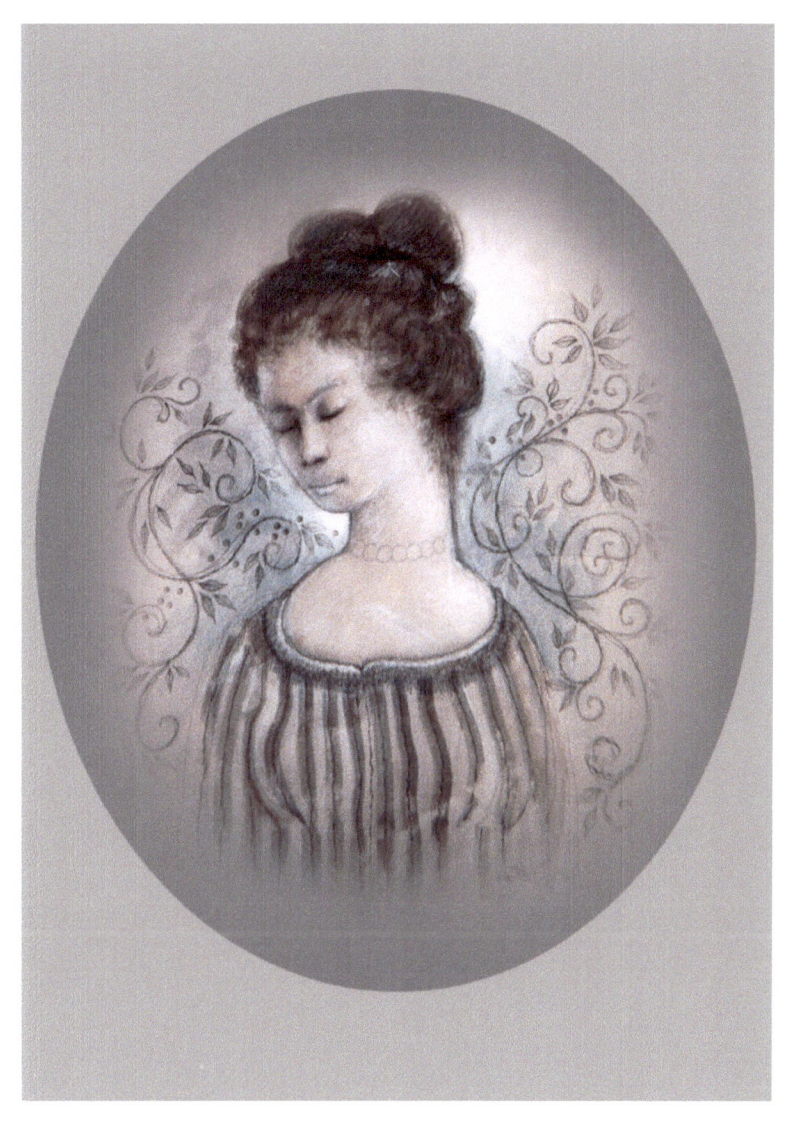

Watercolor.
68.

*

**It is smart to begin a painting with
large and simple objects and end
it with the fine and complicated objects.
Paint from the general to the specific.**

*

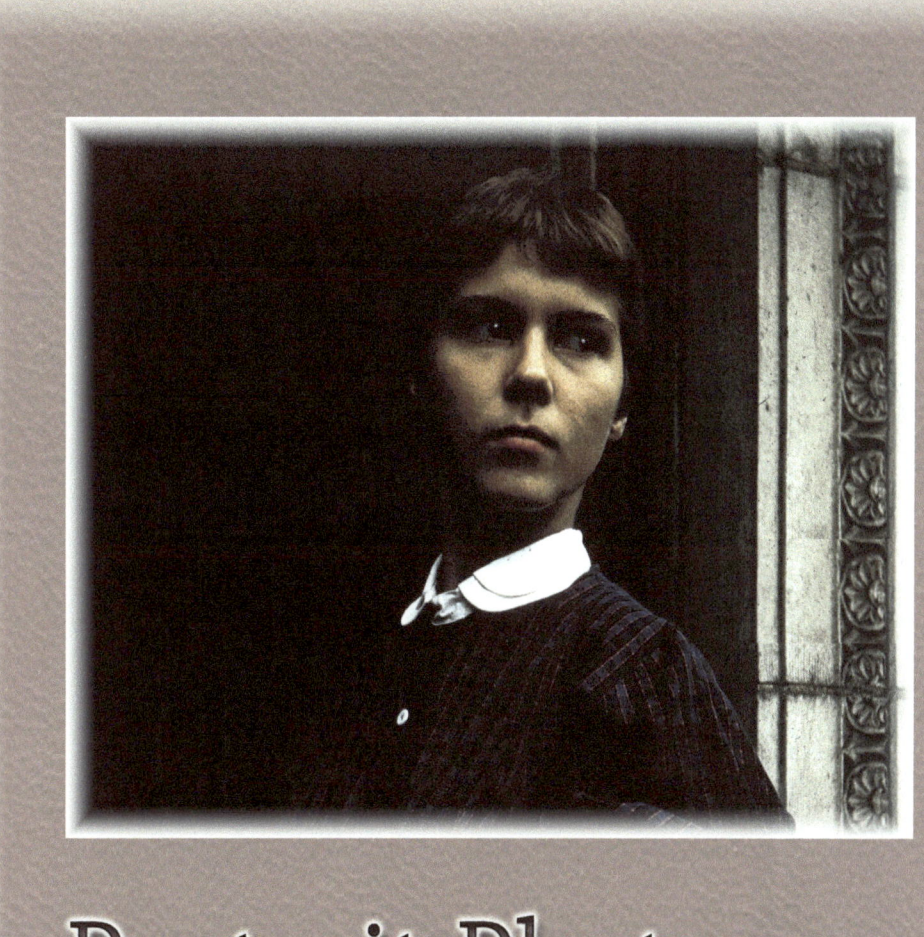

Portrait Photo.

69.

*

The need to compose a work of art comes
from the human need to organize our
world in order to make it functional.
Creation requires an orderly procedure;
distraction involves chaos and the
negation of structure and order.
The point I wish to make is that a sense
of order [composition] is instinctual.

*

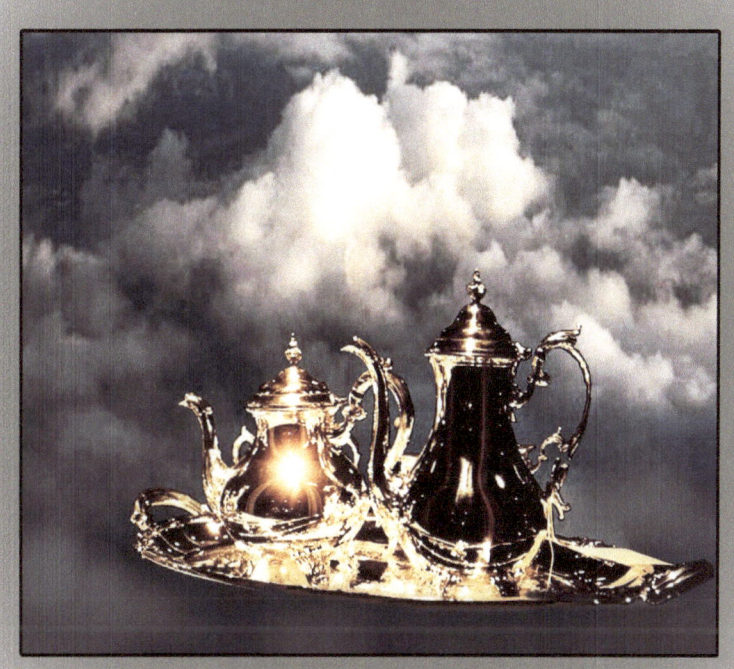

Photo Collage.

70.

*

Be careful with the use of detail.
It can weaken a painting by destroying
its large architectural structure.
Put another way, fragmentation weakens form.
It is similar to the difference between
a large boulder and a pile of gravel.

*

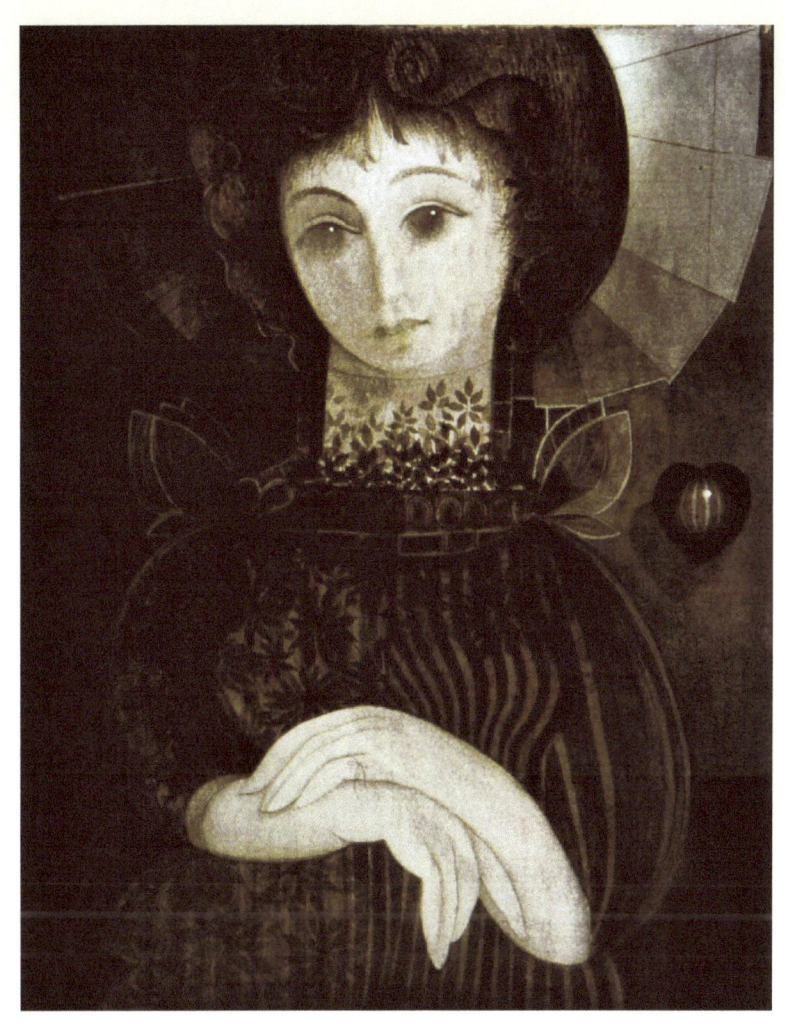

Watercolor.

71.

*

**Never abandon your endless determination
to understand the meaning of art.
Seek its deepest meaning.**

*

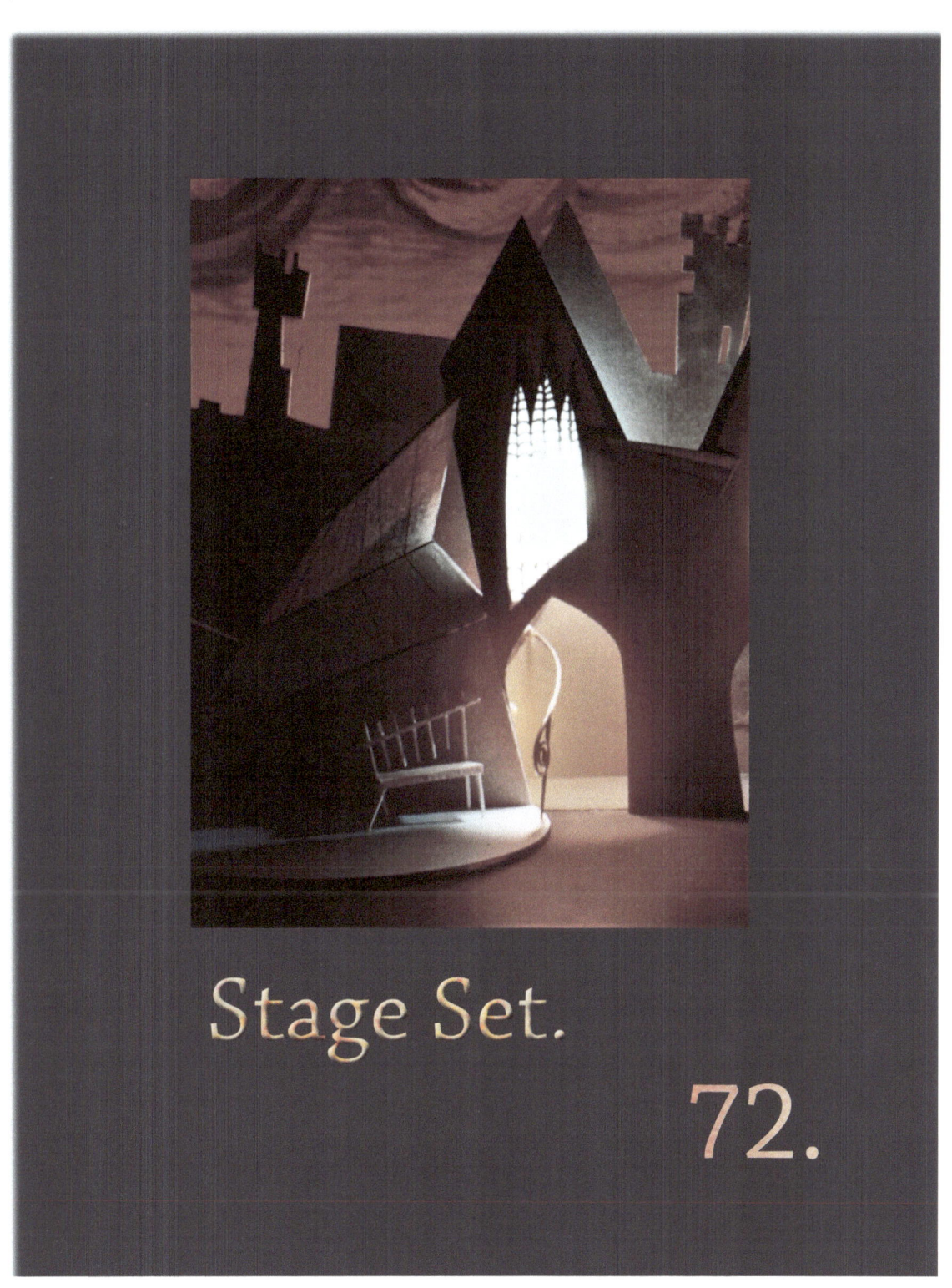

Stage Set.

72.

*

**Never be fooled by the location
where an artist offers his instruction.
A commercial technique is a commercial technique,
whether taught in Cincinnati or in the Bahamas.**

*

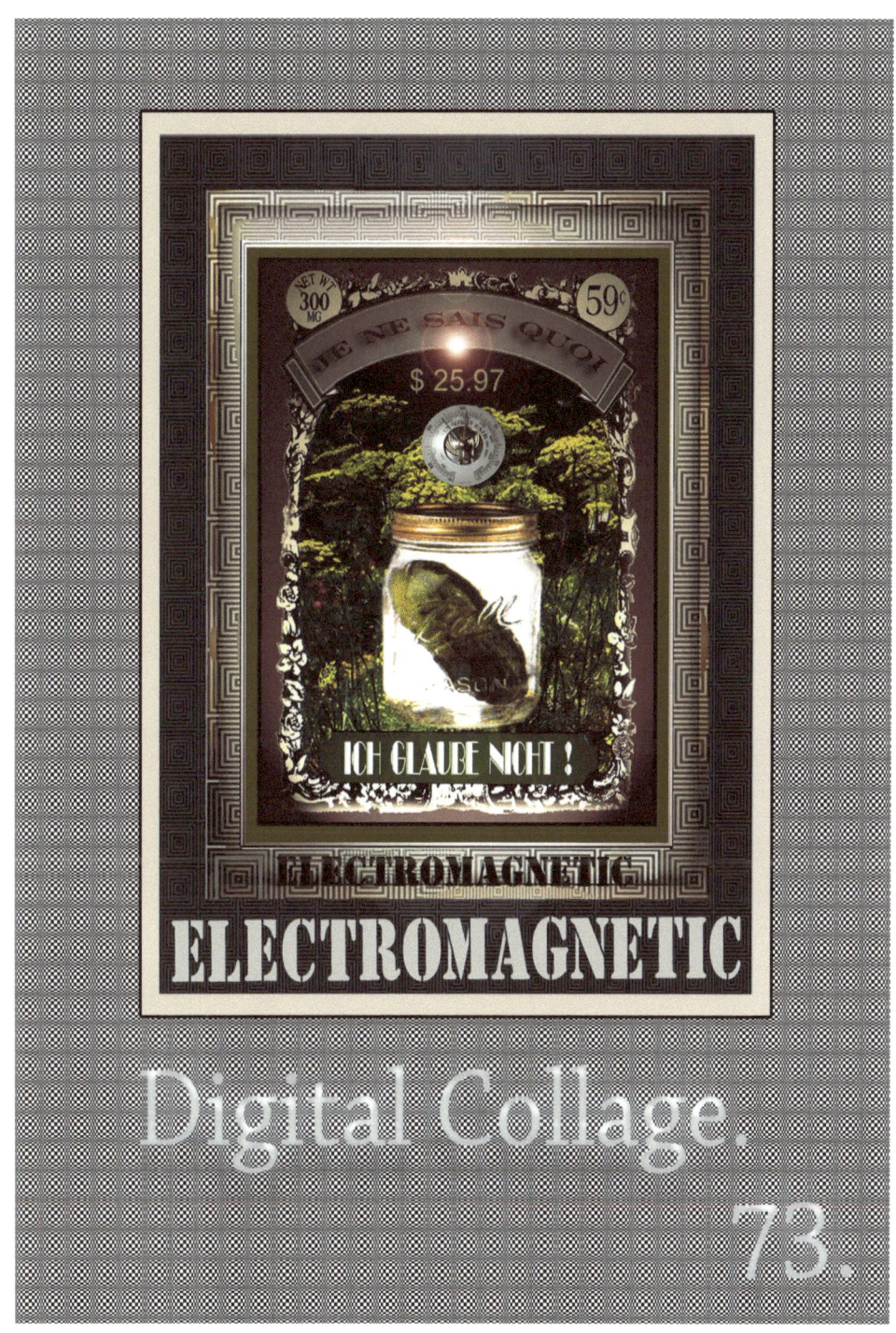

Digital Collage.

73.

*

**A painting may be considered
to be finished when it has unity,
feeling, mystery, beauty, strength,
individuality, and truth.**

*

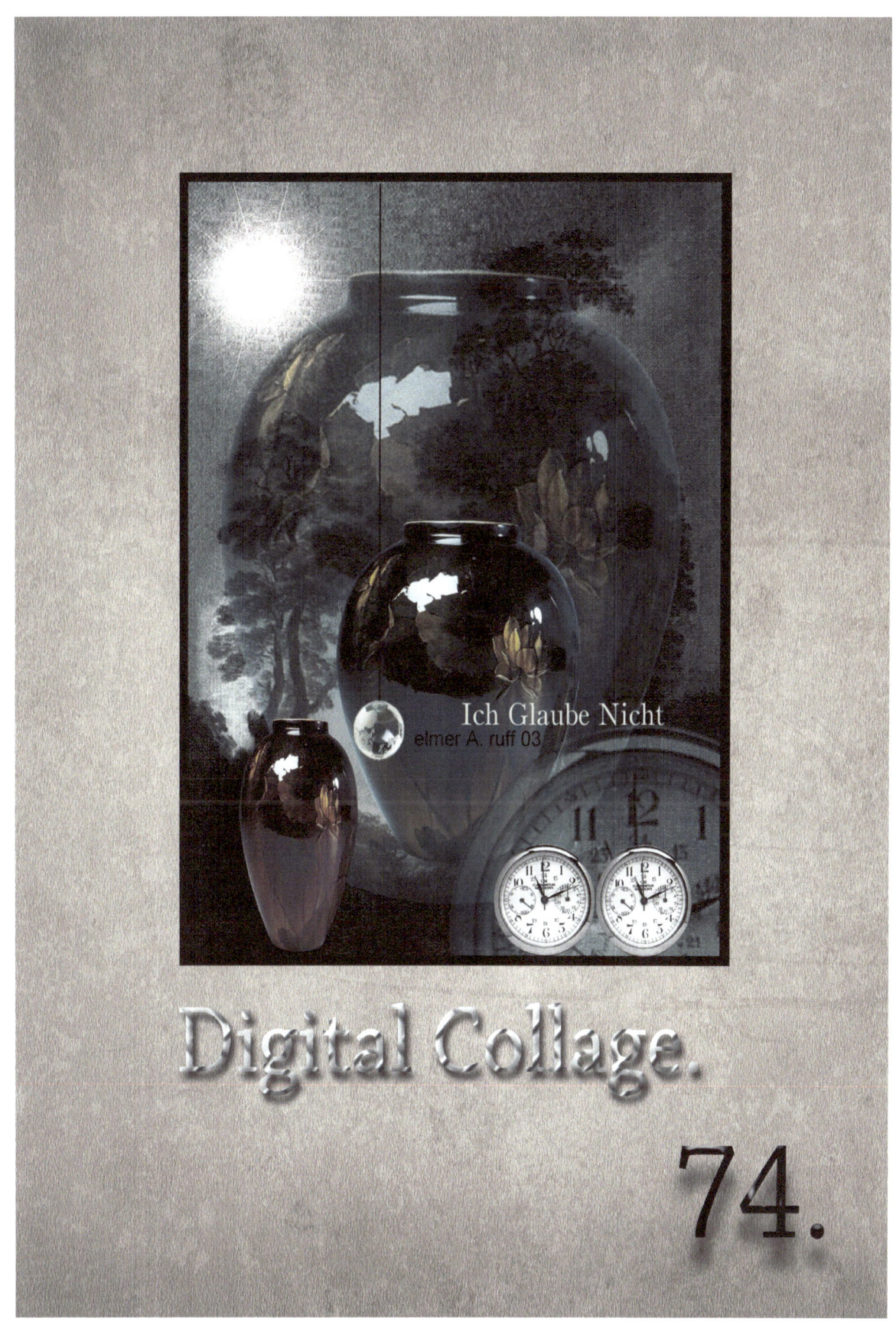

Digital Collage.

74.

*

Painters paint because they must.
Art is a part of their lives.
Painting can be a compulsion as well.

*

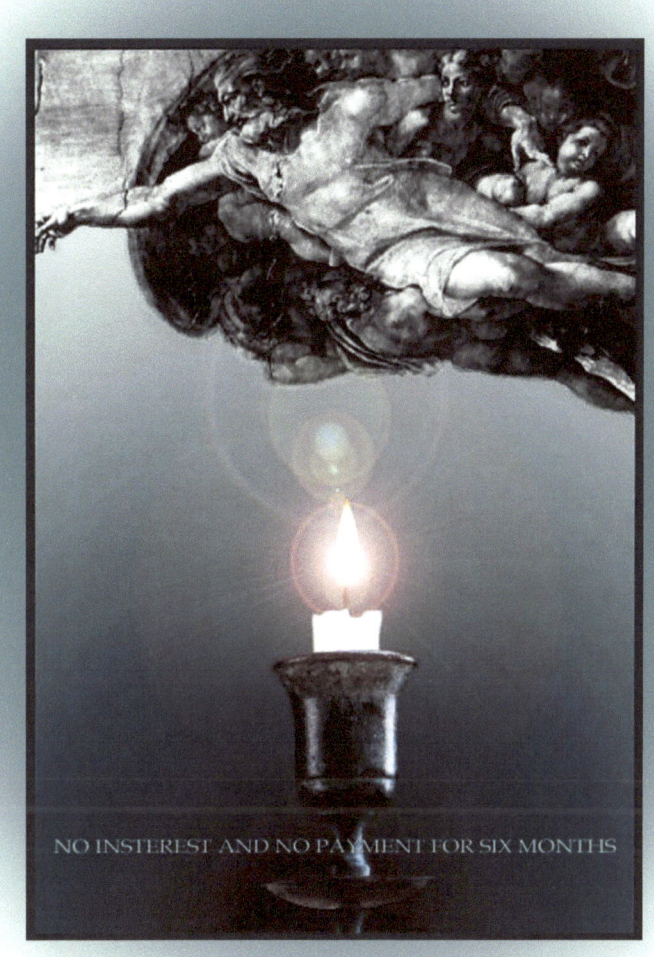

NO INSTEREST AND NO PAYMENT FOR SIX MONTHS

Digital Collage.

75.

*

**Take time to read all you can find about
Gestalt psychology as it concerns art.
This is the best effort ever made
to make a science of art.**

*

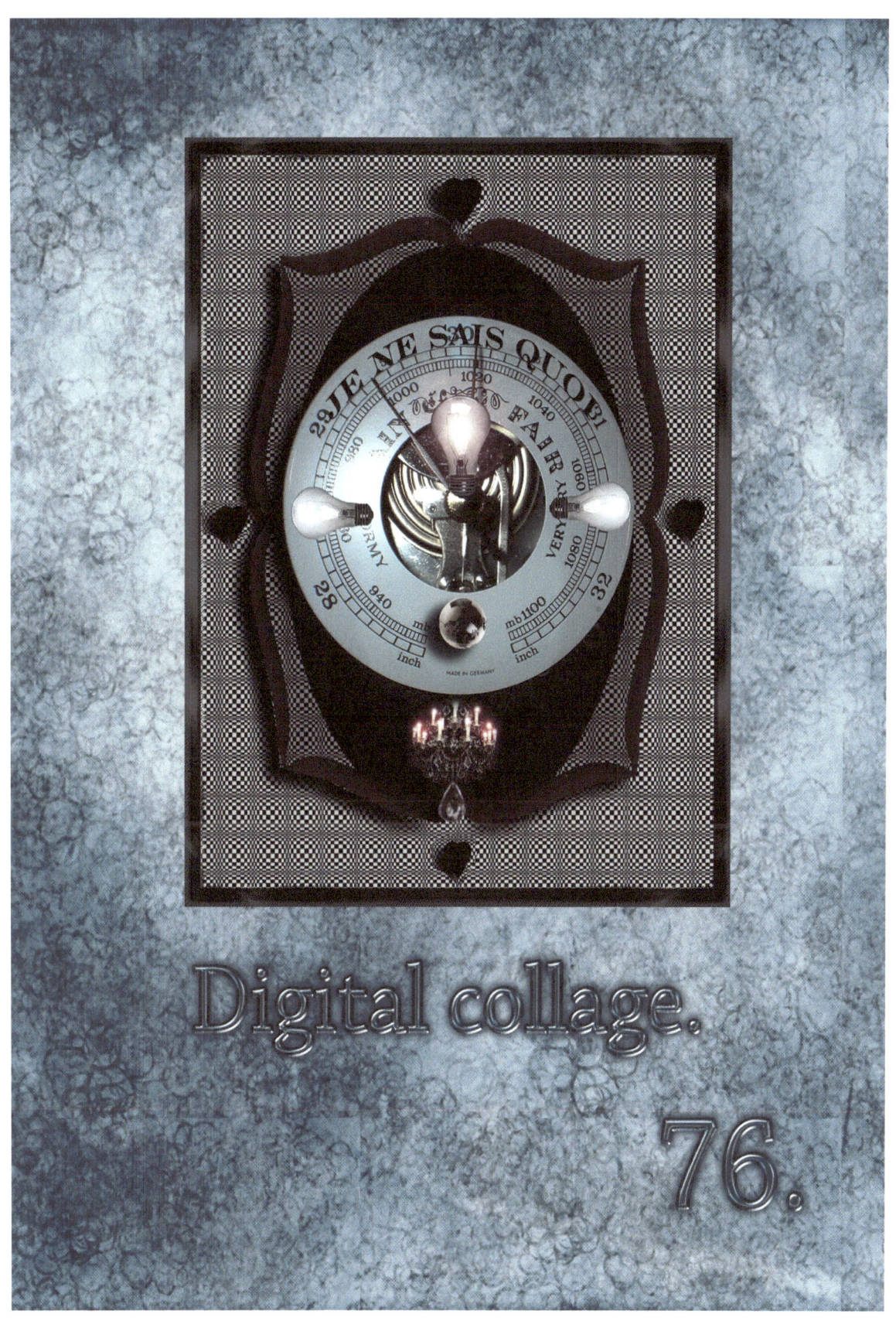

Digital collage.

76.

*

**I strongly recommend that each person
interested in painting also work in collage.
This will improve a sense of structure,
order, design, and stimulate the imagination.**

*

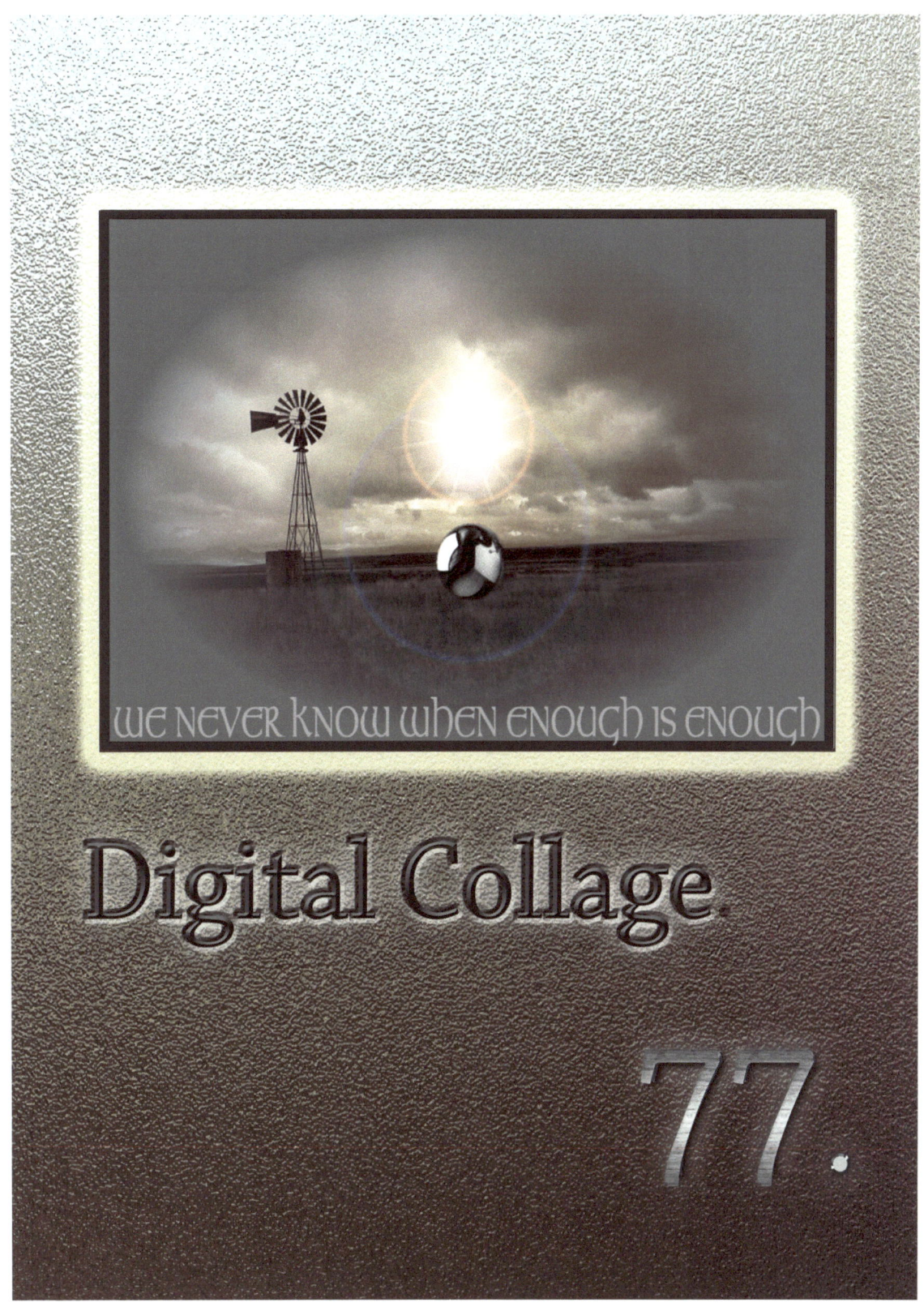

WE NEVER KNOW WHEN ENOUGH IS ENOUGH

Digital Collage.

77.

*

**When fatigued, quit painting.
Fatigue can ruin a work.**

*

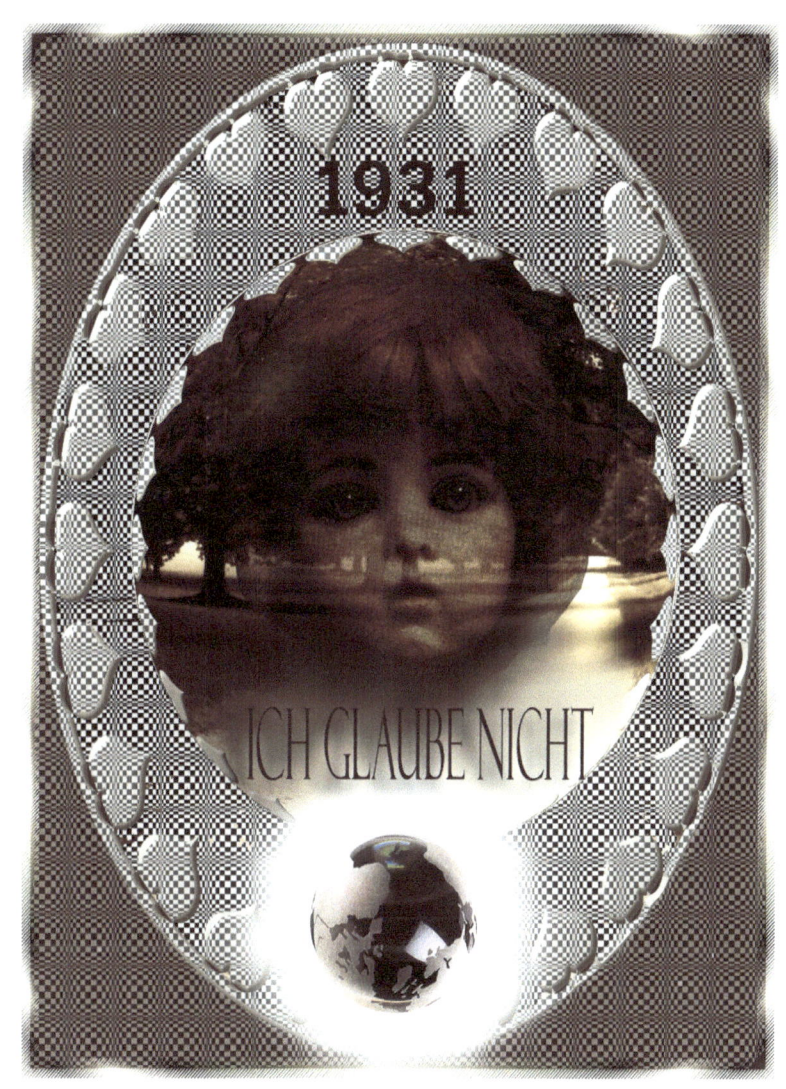

1931

ICH GLAUBE NICHT

Digital Collage.

78.

*

**It is wise when beginning a painting to start
in an area of your work that is not critical.
Always work for a while before taking on difficult parts.**

*

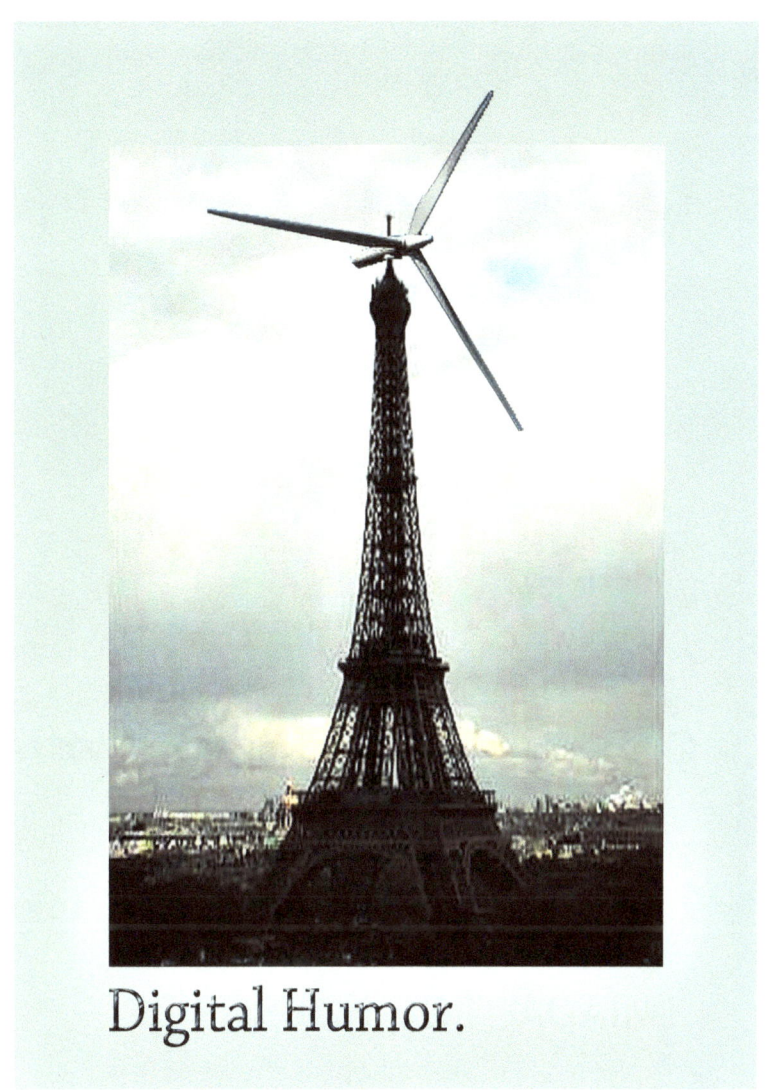

Digital Humor.

79.

*

A wash is a transparent layer of any water-based media.

*

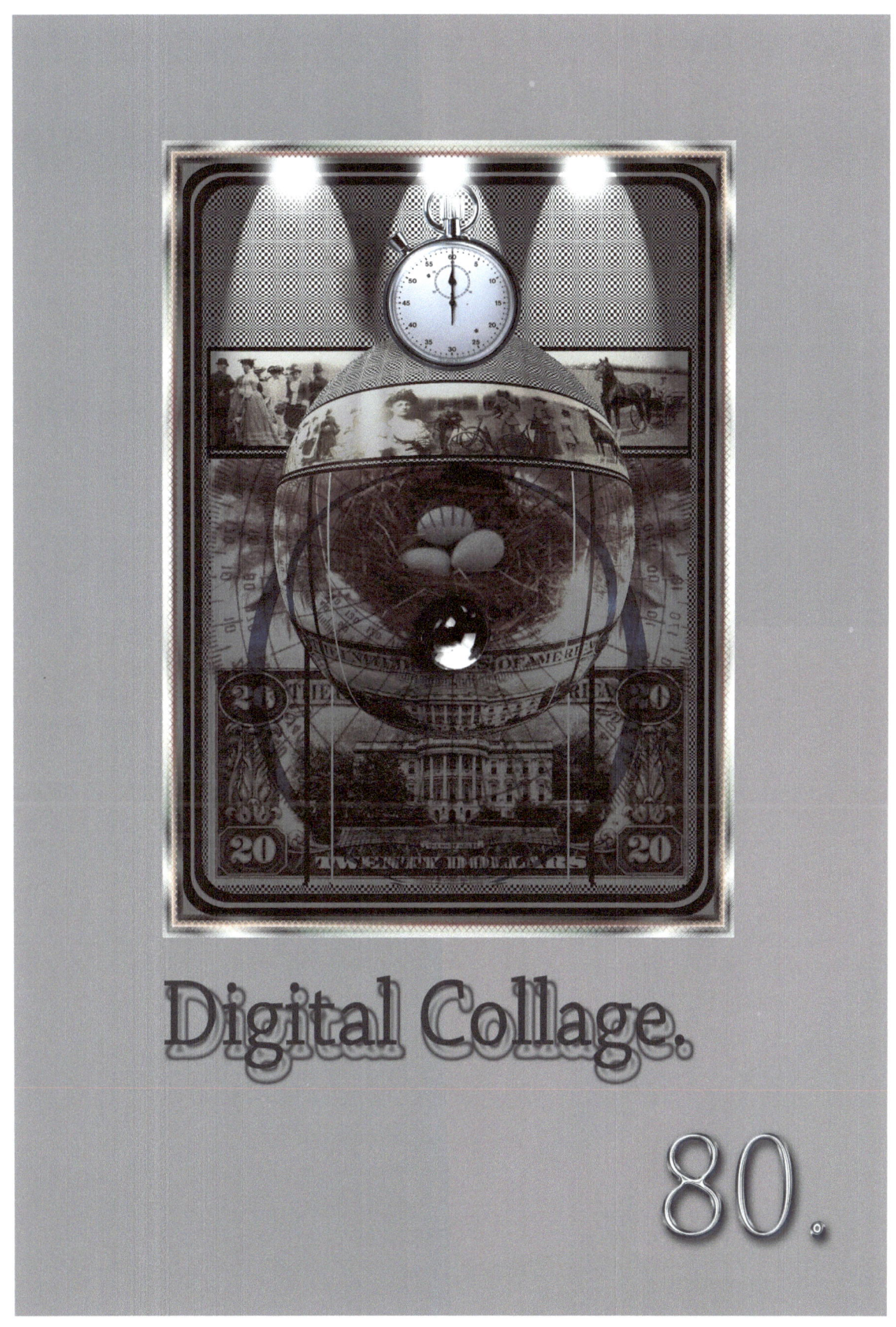

Digital Collage.

80.

*

**A glaze is a transparent layer of oil paint.
The term may be used with acrylic as well.**

*

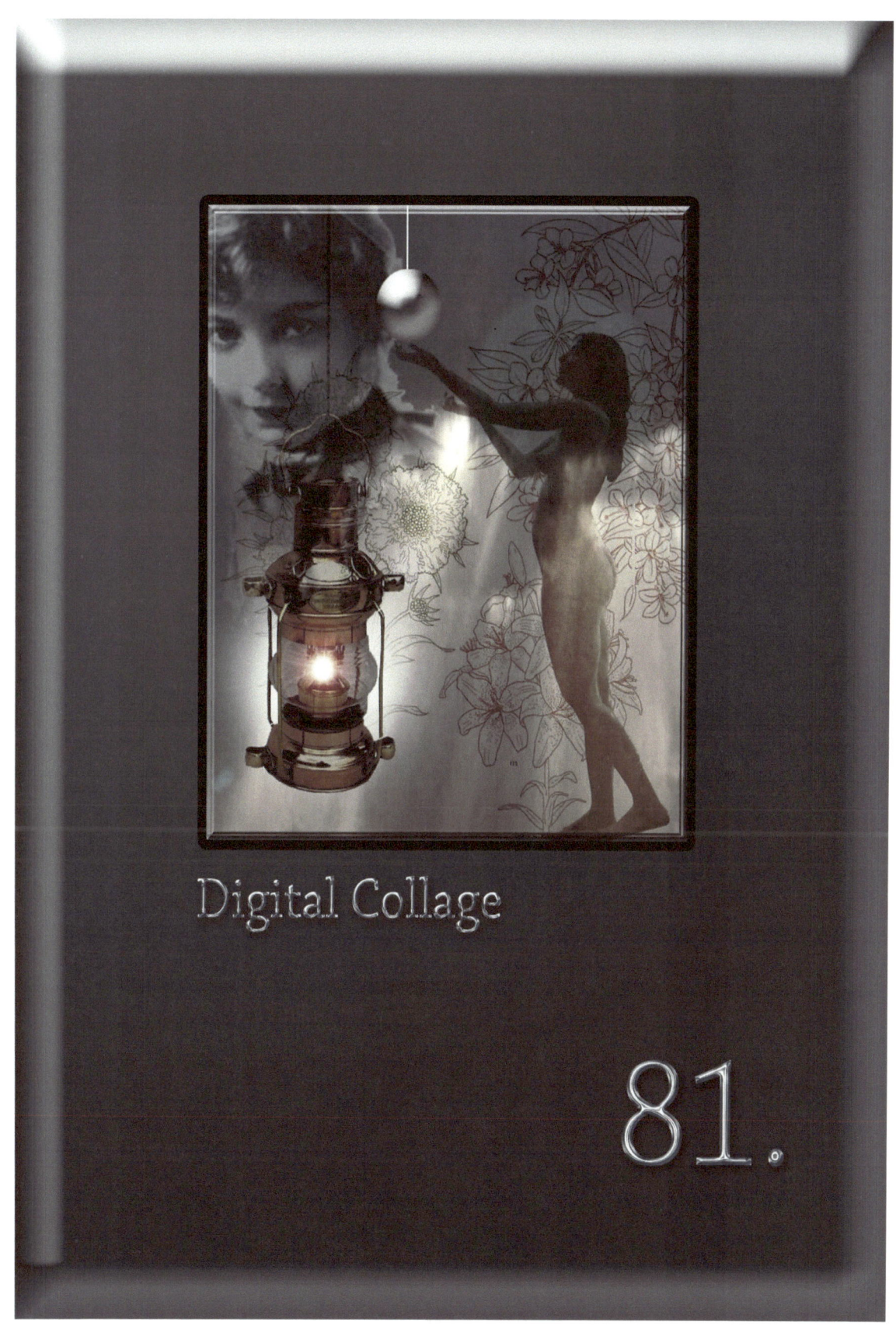

Digital Collage

81.

*

**Realistically, the price of a painting depends
on what someone is willing to pay for it.**

*

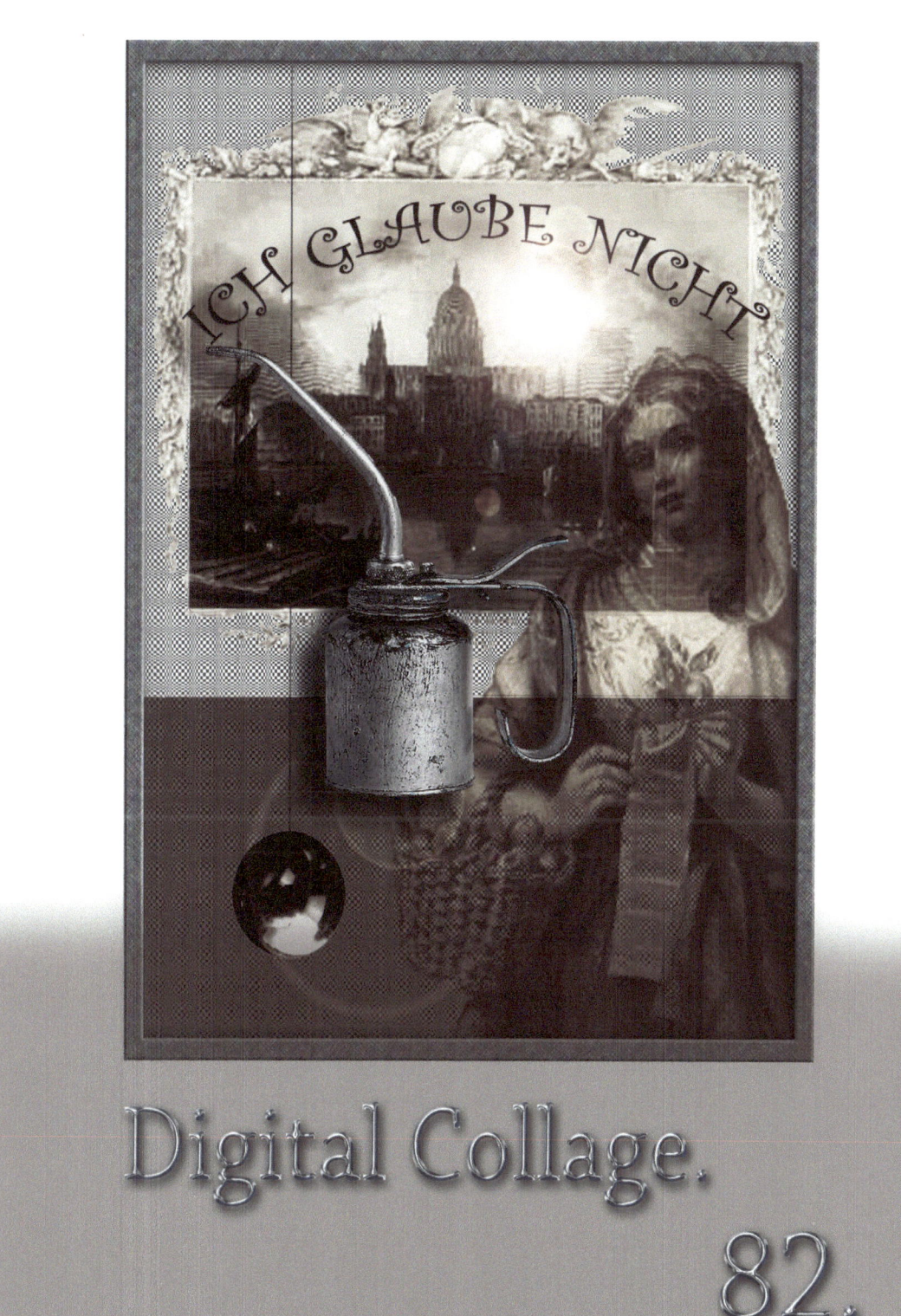

Digital Collage.

82.

*

**The value of a work is another matter.
Value depends on quality, rarity,
condition, demand, and unfortunately,
the reputation of the painter.**

*

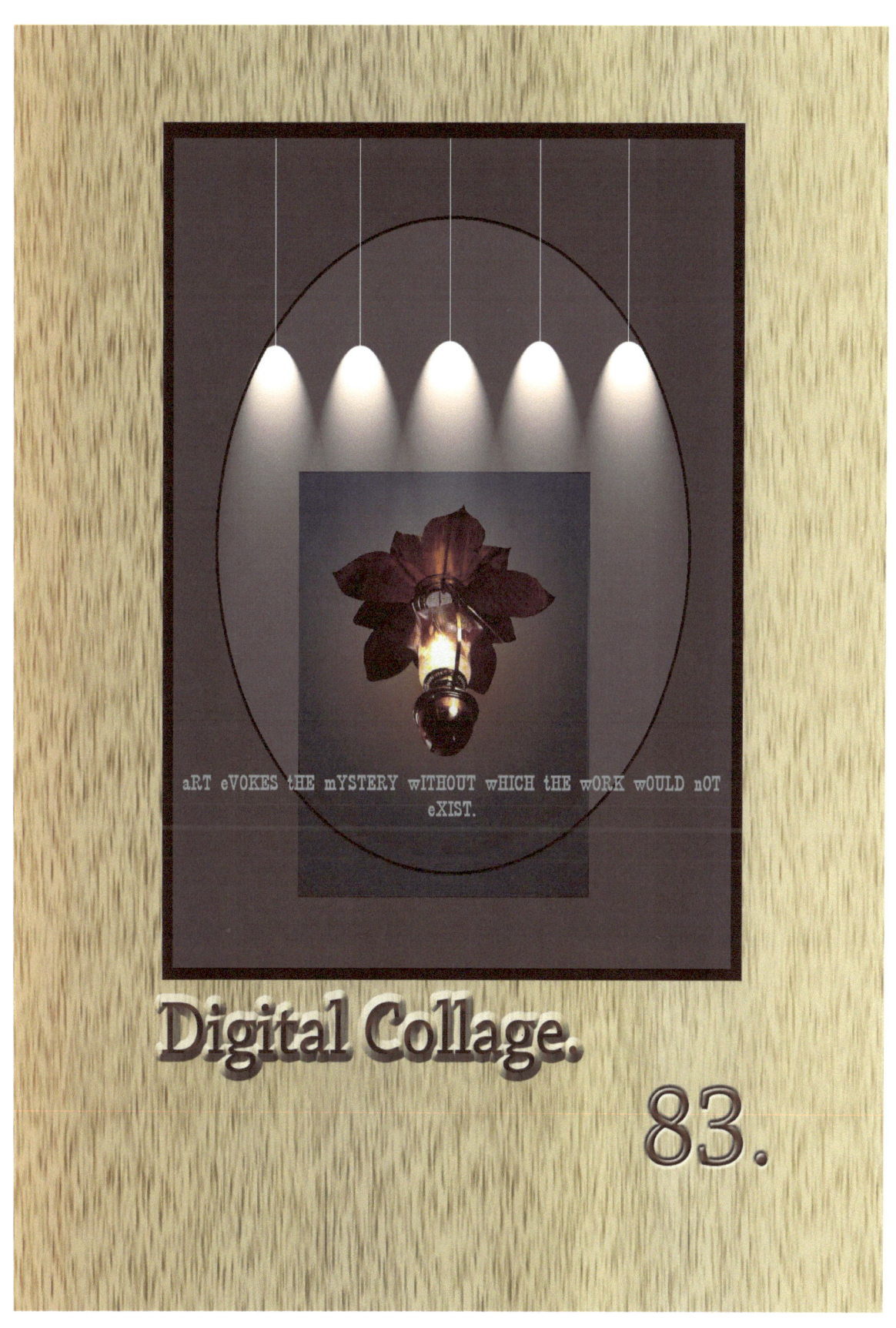

aRT eVOKES tHE mYSTERY wITHOUT wHICH tHE wORK wOULD nOT eXIST.

Digital Collage.

83.

*

In an ideal world, the value of a work should depend solely on its intrinsic qualities and nothing else.

*

\.

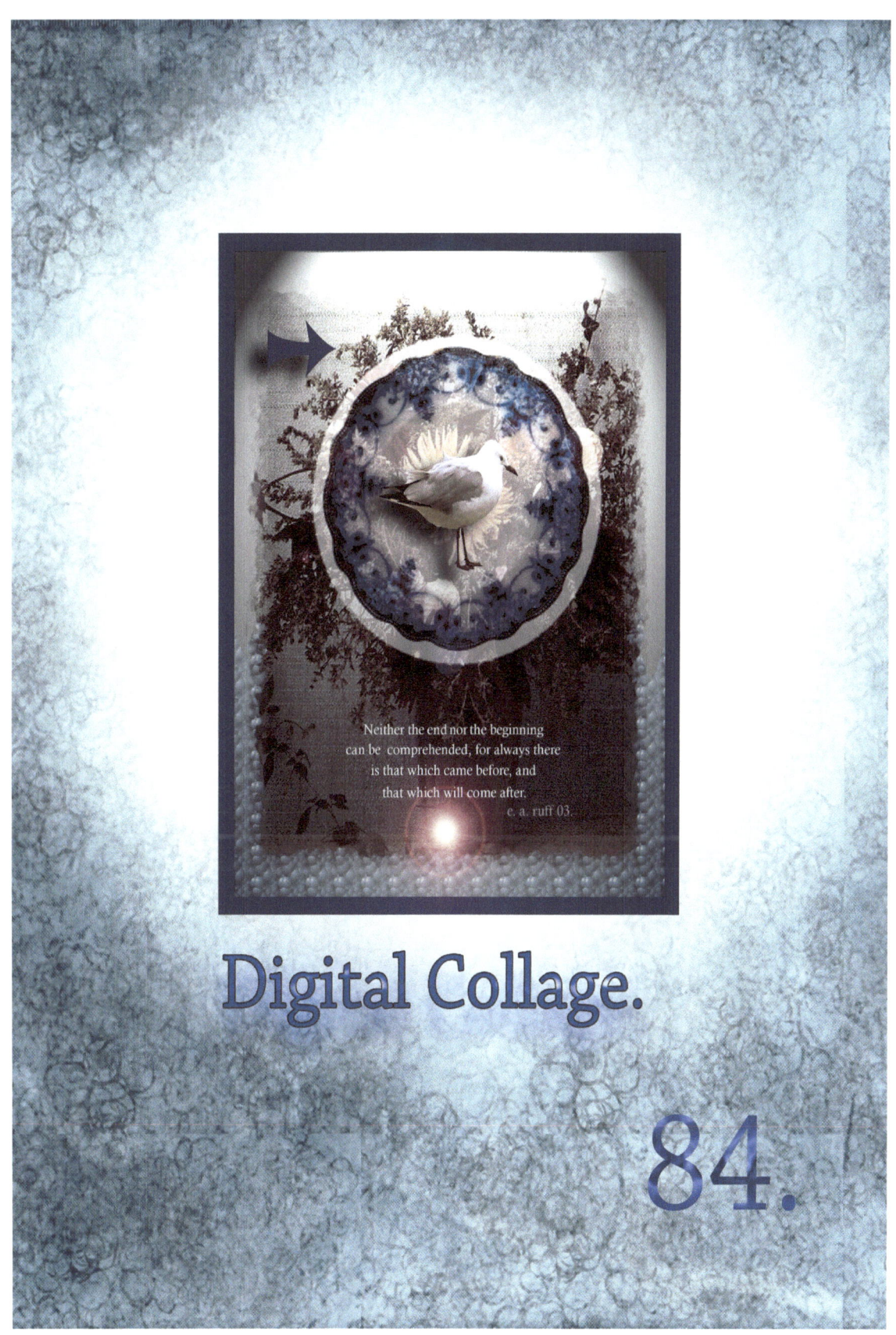

Neither the end nor the beginning
can be comprehended, for always there
is that which came before, and
that which will come after.

e. a. ruff 03.

Digital Collage.

84.

*

**The term "lift" refers to the process of
moistening and blotting a watercolor
in order to remove some of the pigment.**

*

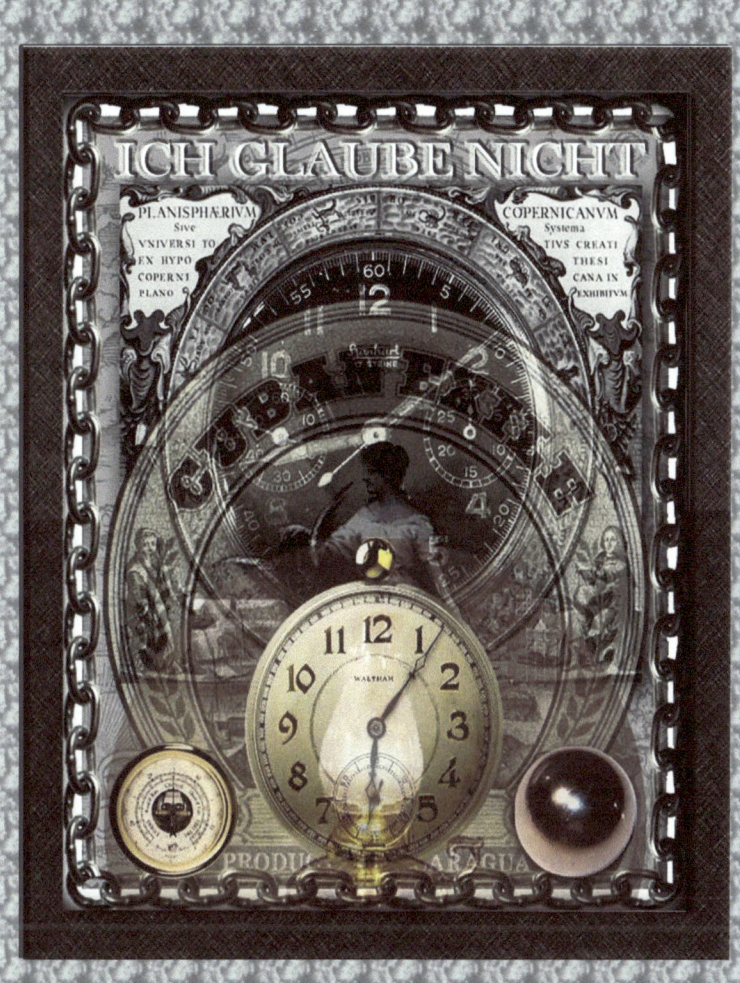

Digital Collage.

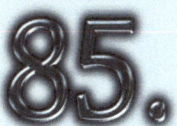

*

Where reason ends, imagination begins.

*

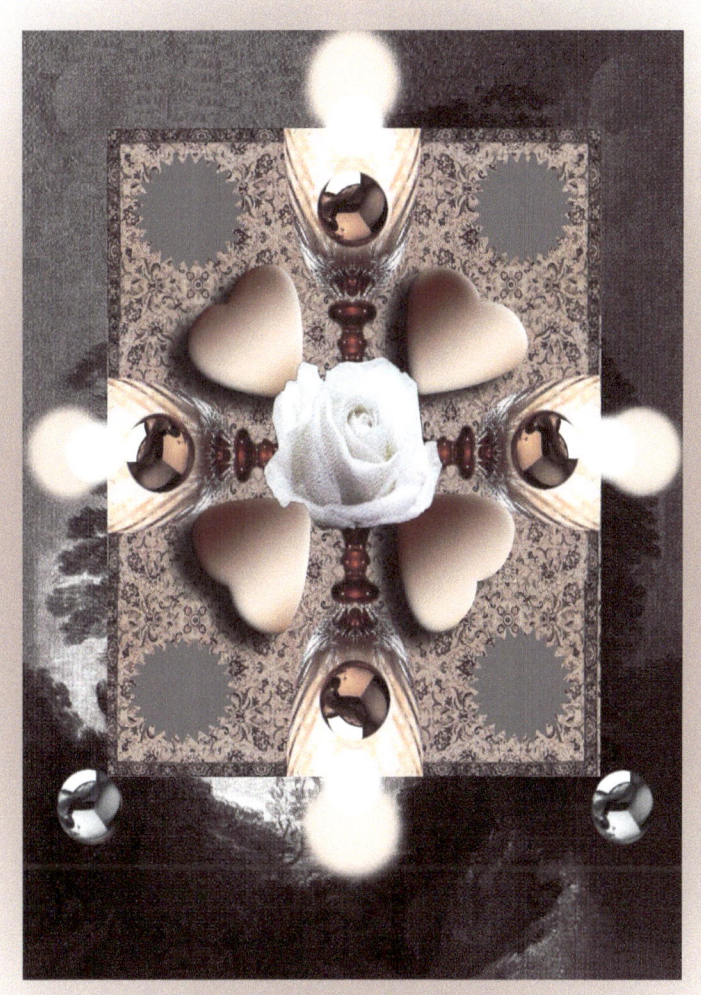

Digital Collage.

86.

*

**Often, what we are unable to understand,
we invent answers for.**

*

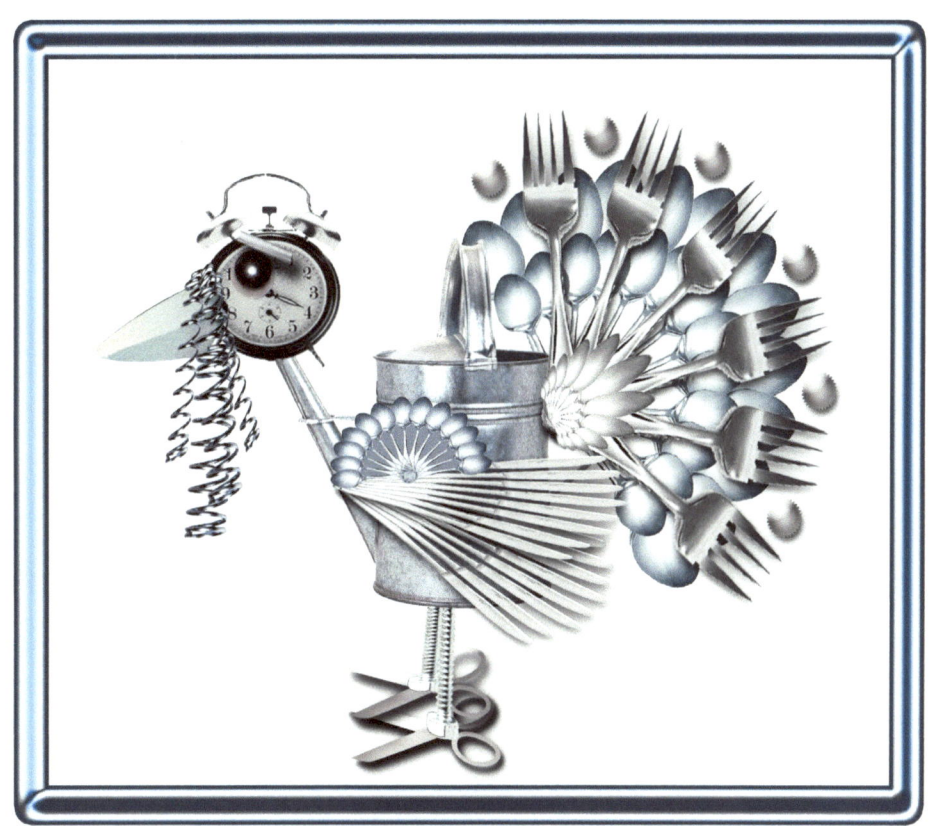

Digital Humor.

87.

*

**Imagination is a normal function of our brain.
Ingenuity involves the imagination.
The true meaning of genius is ingenuity.
It is not what we know, but how we use
what we know that determines genius.**

*

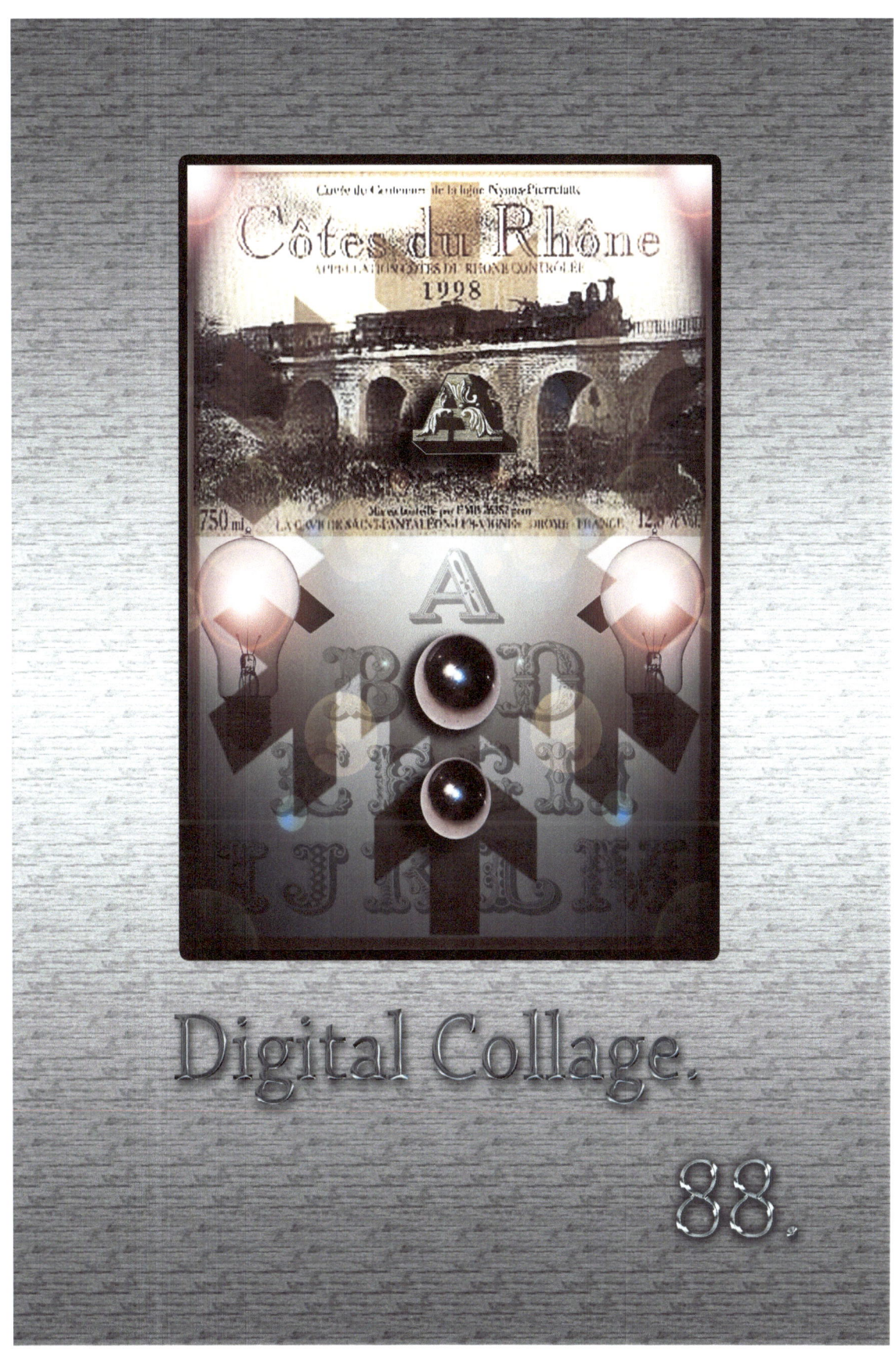

Digital Collage.

88.

*

**Try to strive for ingenuity in your work, as
that will give it individuality and your identity.**

*

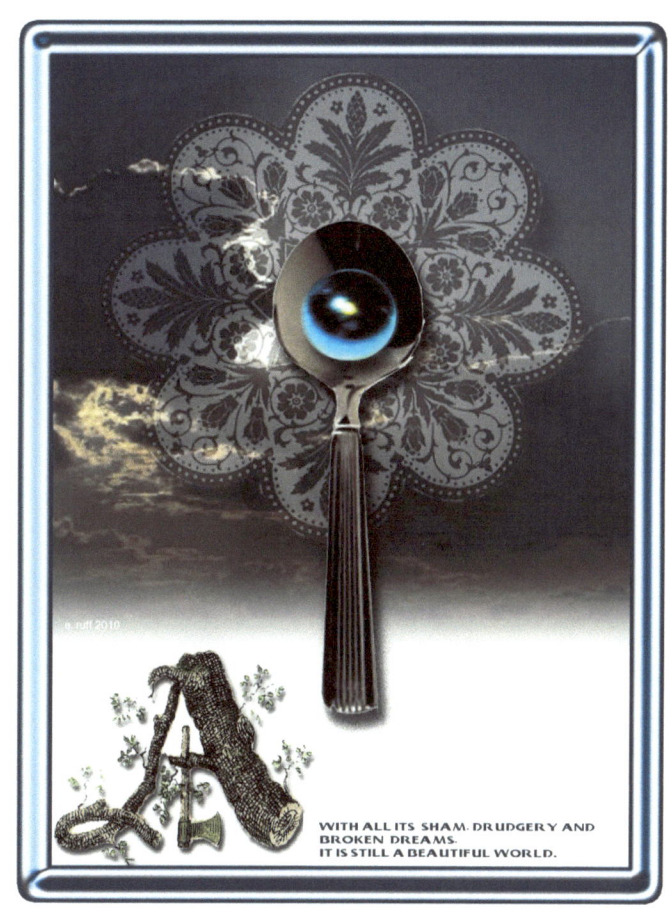

WITH ALL ITS SHAM, DRUDGERY AND
BROKEN DREAMS.
IT IS STILL A BEAUTIFUL WORLD.

Digital Collage.

89.

*

It may not be reasonable in terms
of logic, but great art has life.
It lives, not because of realism
but something much more elusive.
It is endowed with life by the artist's own spirit.
It is a wonderful creative experience
when we feel our paintings come to life.
When a painting achieves this magic,
we often wonder whether we were
responsible for having created it.
Perhaps some other spirit was involved.
*

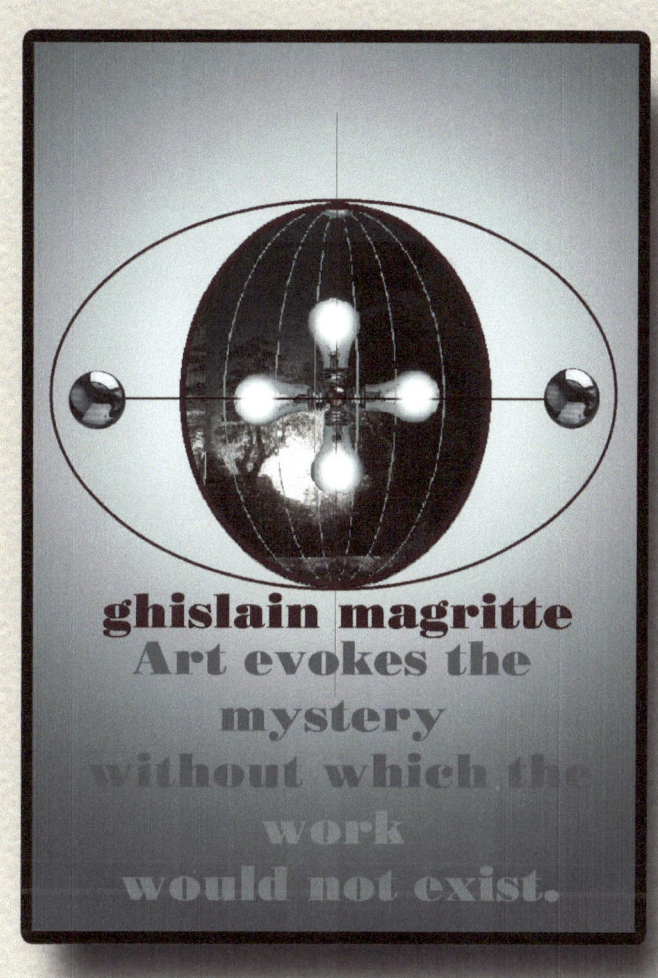

ghislain magritte
Art evokes the
mystery
without which the
work
would not exist.

Digital Collage.

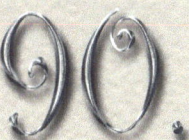

*

It is important to remember that when painting with watercolor not to over-manipulate the paint, for it is a fragile medium and will not tolerate physical abuse. Use soft brushes and a light stroke to minimize melting. Allow separate applications to gather together.

*

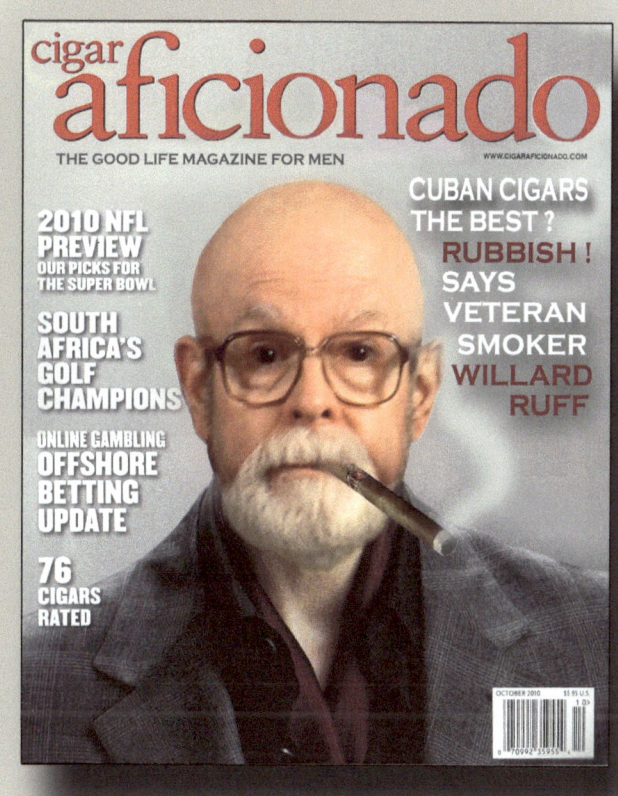

Digital Collage.
Humor.

91.